Published
April 1979

Raymond Carver

D1125866

From the Poetry of Sumer

UNA'S LECTURES

Una's Lectures, delivered annually on the Berkeley campus, memorialize Una Smith, who received her B.S. in History from Berkeley in 1911 and her M.A. in 1913. They express her esteem for the humanities in enlarging the scope of the individual mind. When appropriate, books deriving from the Una's lectureship are published by the University of California Press:

1. *The Resources of Kind: Genre-Theory in the Renaissance,* by Rosalie L. Colie. 1973
2. *From the Poetry of Sumer: Creation, Glorification, Adoration* by Samuel Noah Kramer. 1979

SAMUEL NOAH KRAMER

From the Poetry of Sumer
Creation, Glorification, Adoration

UNIVERSITY OF CALIFORNIA PRESS
Berkeley · Los Angeles · London

PS
4045
.K7

University of California Press
Berkeley and Los Angeles, California
University of California Press, Ltd.
London, England
Copyright © 1979 by
The Regents of the University of California
ISBN 0-520-03703-0
Library of Congress Catalog Card Number: 78-57312
Printed in the United States of America

1 2 3 4 5 6 7 8 9

GREENWOOD LIBRARY
LONGWOOD UNIVERSITY
REDFORD & RACE STREET
FARMVILLE, VA 23909

Contents

I

Sumerian Literature: Recovery and Restoration

One of the major contributions of our century to the humanities is the recovery and restoration of the Sumerian literary works inscribed on tablets from the early second millennium B.C., which constitute the oldest written literature of significant quantity and quality as yet uncovered by the archeological spade. Sumerian myths and epic tales, hymns and laments, essays and disputations, proverbs and precepts, now serve as prime source material for the historian of literature and religion, for Biblical and classical scholars, for anthropologists and sociologists. I will present here a panoramic review of the recovery and restoration over the past hundred years of this long-buried and completely forgotten literature, and I will even venture to predict the promise of the future.

It was in the year 1875, just over a century ago, that the British Museum published volume four of the magnificent five-volume series entitled *Inscriptions of Western Asia*, conceived, planned, and edited by Henry Rawlinson, the "father of Assyriology." The texts in this volume, now known to all cuneiformists as 4R, were copied by the renowned British archeologist and epigraphist George Smith.[1] They consist primarily of bilinguals, that is, they are written in the Sumerian language with a line-by-line translation into the Semitic tongue now generally designated as Akkadian,

1. A second edition of this volume with numerous additions and corrections by Th. G. Pinches was published in 1891.

1

but known formerly as Assyrian or Babylonian. These 4R bilinguals all come from the Ashurbanipal library excavated by A. H. Layard at Nineveh, and can thus be dated to the seventh century B.C. The majority of these Ashurbanipal bilinguals are incantations, but scattered among them are several fragmentary poetic chants relating to the cults of the goddess Inanna (the Semitic Ishtar) and her doomed lover Dumuzi (the Biblical Tammuz) as well as a literary "catalogue," that is, a tablet inscribed with an itemized list of the titles—the incipits—of numerous Sumerian literary works known to the Semitic Ashurbanipal scribes.[2] And thus it was that the first inkling of the existence of a Sumerian literature reached the modern scholarly world.

Six years after the appearance of 4R, in the year 1881/1882, the noted German cuneiformist Paul Haupt published a volume entitled *Akkadische und sumerische Keilschrifttexte*, consisting of texts from the Ashurbanipal library that he had copied in the British Museum, and among these are several Sumero-Akkadian literary bilinguals, including a hymn of considerable length to the goddess Inanna. Fifteen years later, in 1896, another German scholar, George Reisner, published the epoch-making *Sumerisch-babylonische Hymnen nach Tontafeln griechischer Zeit*, which includes copies of a large number of Sumero-Akkadian literary bilinguals from the Berlin museums, primarily liturgical laments, some of which duplicate pieces published by George Smith and Paul Haupt. It thus became evident that there must have existed a body of Sumerian literary works which the Semitic scribes copied from Sumerian originals, and to which they appended translations into their own language. But none of the Sumerian originals had as yet been recovered, and their existence was only a matter of surmise.[3] Moreover, even assuming that they did exist, there was no

2. This catalogue has been edited by a number of scholars; for the most recent, see Joachim Krecher, *Sumerische Kultlyrik* (1966), pp. 19–21 (note 9).

3. To be sure, the existence of an ancient Sumerian literature became known as early as 1884, with the publication of Ernest de Sarzec's *Decouvertes en Chaldée*, which included two long multifaceted poetic compositions commemorating Gudea's rebuilding of the Eninnu temple in Lagash, inscribed on two terra-cotta

way of knowing when they were written, except that this must have been earlier than the Ashurbanipal bilinguals, that is, earlier than the seventh century B.C. Not unexpectedly the resolution of both these matters was provided by the British Museum.

In 1902 there appeared volume 15 of the series commonly known as *CT* (*Cuneiform Texts from Babylonian Tablets in the British Museum*), consisting of copies of a considerable number of tablets prepared by L. W. King, then Assistant Keeper in the museum. Among these are copies of sixteen well-preserved tablets inscribed with unilingual Sumerian compositions concerned with various Sumerian deities, some of which were designated by the ancient scribe himself as *irshemma*, that is, a lamentful song (*ir*) accompanied by a drumlike musical instrument known in Sumerian as *shem*.[4] The contents of these Sumerian unilinguals are so similar to the bilinguals published by Smith, Haupt, and Reisner that they left no doubt that they were the type of Sumerian original which the Akkadian scribes had before them when preparing their translations. As for the date of Sumerian unilinguals published in *CT* 15, their script was readily recognizable as that of the period in Mesopotamian history commonly known as Old Babylonian, extending from about 2000 to 1650 B.C.; they were thus more than a millennium older than the Ashurbanipal bilinguals.

Still these relatively few unilingual compositions with their rather brief, lamentful content could hardly be taken as conclusive proof of the existence of a large, complex, variegated literature. The conviction that there existed such a literature grew gradually in the course of the decades that followed with the accumulation of evidence that derived primarily from three sources: (1) the publica-

---

cylinders of considerable size. However, the compositions inscribed on these Gudea Cylinders differed so materially, in both content and form, from the Sumerian text of the published bilinguals that it was difficult to perceive any significant relationship between them.

4. The *irshemma* is a melancholy literary genre bemoaning the destruction of a city and its temples, or the suffering and death of a deity, usually the deified Dumuzi; for full details, see a forthcoming study by Mark Cohen, who has devoted several years of research to this Sumerian literary genre.

tion of copies of many of the several thousand Sumerian literary tablets and fragments excavated at Nippur by the University of Pennsylvania between the years 1889 and 1900,[5] beginning in 1909 with Hugo Radau's "Miscellaneous Texts from the Temple Library of Nippur"[6] and continuing in one form or another to the present day; (2) the publication of more than three hundred tablets and fragments of unknown provenance from the purchased collections of the Berlin Staatliche Museen, the Louvre, and the British Museum; and (3) the publication of some five hundred tablets and fragments excavated by Henri de-Genouillac at Kish and by Leonard Woolley at Ur.

The major publications of Sumerian unilingual texts from the Old Babylonian period may be itemized decade by decade as follows:

The years 1911–1920 were rich vintage years that saw the publication of twelve volumes concerned with the Sumerian literary documents. Two of these appeared in the very first year of the decade, in 1911, with copies of a score of tablets and fragments from the Nippur collection of the University Museum: (1) D. W. Myhrman's *Babylonian Hymns and Prayers*, particularly noteworthy for the inclusion of the upper half of a six-column tablet inscribed with the first half of the myth "Inanna and Enki: The Transfer of the *me* from Eridu to Erech";[7] and (2) Hugo Radau's *Sumerian Hymns and Prayers to the God Nin-ib*, which consisted of texts revolving about the god Ninurta.

5. These are now located in approximately equal portions in the Museum of the Ancient Orient in Istanbul and in the University Museum in Philadelphia.

6. This important pioneering publication of some of the Sumerian literary documents in the University Museum appeared in the *Hilprecht Anniversary Volume* (1909), pp. 374–457.

7. This "charter" myth, celebrating the rise of Erech as one of Sumer's great political and religious centers, was edited and published in 1975 by Gertrud Farber-Flügge, who began the relevant research in the University Museum in a monograph entitled *Der Mythos "Inanna und Enki" unter besonderer Berüksüchtigung der Liste der Me*. For the difficult and complex theological concept denoted by the word *me*, see pp. 45–46, this volume.

One year later, in 1912, Heinrich Zimmern published the first volume of *Sumerische Kultlieder aus altbabylonischer Zeit*, with copies and photographs of one hundred tablets and fragments from the tablet collection of the Berlin Staatliche Museen, some of which were large multicolumn tablets inscribed with a varied assortment of liturgical laments and dirges, and not a few of which revolved about the god Dumuzi.[8] In the very next year, 1913, Zimmern published the second volume of *Sumerische Kultlieder* with copies of another hundred or so Sumerian literary pieces, this time mostly fragments. This same year Hugo Radau published thirteen tablets and fragments from the Nippur collection of the University Museum inscribed with a varied assortment of Dumuzi texts in his *Sumerian Hymns and Prayers to the God Dumuzi*, and Stephen Langdon published his *Babylonian Liturgies*, which included copies of more than two hundred fragments, mostly from the Ashurbanipal library.

In the following year, 1914, appeared Arno Poebel's superb *Historical and Grammatical Texts*, which actually should have been entitled *Historical, Literary, and Grammatical Texts* since it includes copies of more than a score of Sumerian literary tablets and fragments, among which is a large six-column tablet inscribed with the second half of the myth "Inanna and Enki: The Transfer of the *me* from Eridu to Erech" (the first half was inscribed on the fragmentary six-column tablet published by Myhrman three years before), as well as three extracts from the myth "Inanna's Descent to the Nether World"[9] (the Sumerian forerunner of the Akkadian "Ishtar's Descent to the Nether World," which had become known

8. Most of these are written in a phonetic nonhistorical orthography that obscures the reading and meaning of many of the words and phrases, and it is only in recent years that a breakthrough has been made, at least to some extent, in the translation and interpretation of these important documents. For fuller details, see my *The Sacred Marriage Rite* (1969), p. 158, note 6, and especially Joachim Krecher's recent publication. (See Assyriological Bibliography in *Orientalia* for relevant items.)

9. For the contents of this myth, see pp. 82–83 of this volume.

to the scholarly world half a century before), not to mention fragments of various other literary genres. And in the very same year, 1914, Stephen Langdon published his *Historical and Religious Texts from the Temple Library of Nippur*, containing copies of more than fifty pieces from the Nippur collection of the Istanbul Museum of the Ancient Orient.

Stephen Langdon dominated the Sumerian literary scene during the remaining years of the decade with his publication in 1915, 1917, and 1919 respectively of (1) *The Sumerian Epic of Paradise, the Flood, and the Fall of Man;*[10] (2) *Sumerian Liturgical Texts;* and (3) *Sumerian Liturgies and Psalms.* Langdon's copies of the tablets and fragments from the Nippur collection of the University Museum are rather shoddy, and his attempted transliterations and translations are quite unreliable. Nevertheless it should be recognized and appreciated that by making available the texts of close to one hundred tablets and fragments whose contents range over the entire gamut of the Sumerian literary repertoire, Langdon enriched immensely our knowledge of the nature, scope, and significance of Sumerian literature.

Finally, towards the very end of the decade, in 1918, George Barton published his *Miscellaneous Babylonian Inscriptions*, which included copies of eleven tablets and fragments from the Nippur collection of the University Museum. Barton's autographs and translations are even worse than those of Langdon. Nevertheless it is to be acknowledged that he, too, added considerably to the ever-growing stock of essential source material. Moreover he included copies and photographs of a clay cylinder inscribed probably as early as the period of the Dynasty of Akkad with what seems

---

10. Langdon's rather pretentious title for the composition is quite unjustified—the myth has nothing to do with the Flood, or the "Fall of Man," and while it does concern a "Paradise-land," the protagonists are not mortals, like Adam and Eve, but gods and goddesses; for a very brief sketch of the contents of this myth, see pp. 40–41 of this volume.

to be a myth of Enlil and Ninhursag, although most of its contents still remain obscure.[11] What is most significant about this document, however, is that it provided clear evidence for the existence of Sumerian literary works in pre-Gudean days, a surmise that has since been amply corroborated by the archaic Sumerian literary texts excavated recently at Abu Salabih, an ancient site northwest of Nippur.[12]

The decade that followed, the years 1921–1930, was almost as productive as the preceding: it witnessed the publication of eight volumes containing among them copies of more than two hundred tablets and fragments representing virtually every Sumerian literary genre: myths, epic tales, hymns, laments, "Sacred Marriage" songs, essays, disputations, proverbs, and precepts. In 1921 appeared *CT* 36, which included Cyril Gadd's excellent copies of ten well-preserved tablets in the British Museum. In 1923 Stephen Langdon again came on the literary scene with a very important publication of texts from the Weld-Blundell collection of the Ashmolean Museum entitled *Sumerian and Semitic Religious and Historical Texts*. In 1924, Edward Chiera, who played a key role in the restoration of Sumerian literature despite his early, untimely death in 1933, published his *Sumerian Religious Texts*, with elegant copies of fifty-three tablets and fragments in the Istanbul Museum of the Ancient Orient. In 1924/1925, Henri de-Genouillac published a considerable number of Sumerian literary pieces, mostly quite fragmentary, in his *Premières recherches archéologiques à Kich*, which gave evidence of the existence of a Sumerian literary repertoire in Kish in northern Sumer similar to that of Nippur in central Sumer. And at the very end of the decade, in 1930, this same scholar published two volumes of *Textes*

11. For the mythological significance of its introductory lines, see p. 28, this volume.

12. See Robert D. Biggs, *Inscriptions from Tell Abu Salabih* (1974), a major, fundamental contribution to the early stages of Sumerian literature.

religieux sumériens du Louvre, containing copies of ninety-eight tablets and fragments that augmented impressively our stock of fundamental source material.[13]

The decade 1931–1940 saw the publication of only two volumes of Sumerian literary texts, Edward Chiera's *Sumerian Epics and Myths* and *Sumerian Texts of Varied Content,* but these contain more than two hundred and fifty pieces, some of which were of very considerable size and immense importance. Chiera had copied them in the University Museum in the 1920s, when he was still a member of the Department of Oriental Studies of the University of Pennsylvania, and later when he was invited by Henry Breasted to become editor-in-chief of the Assyrian Dictionary Project, it was agreed between them that the Oriental Institute would publish these documents. Chiera's unexpected, premature death left these texts, to which he had devoted much time and labor, stranded, as it were, and I was invited by the editorial department of the Oriental Institute to prepare them for posthumous publication. It was in the course of trying to understand the contents of these documents and penetrate their meaning that I became convinced that the restoration, translation, and interpretation of the Sumerian literary works, especially those of any considerable length, would be virtually impossible until many more of the Sumerian literary tablets and fragments lying about in the cupboards of the various museums, and particularly in the Nippur collections of the University Museum and the Museum of the Ancient Orient, were made available to the scholarly world in one form or another. I therefore traveled to Istanbul in 1937, where in the course of the next eighteen months I copied close to two hundred tablets and fragments of wide-ranging literary content. The resulting volume, entitled *Sumerian Literary Texts from Nip-*

13. De-Genouillac's copies are not altogether satisfactory, and a very careful and helpful collation of these texts is now being prepared by J. Durand of the École Pratique des Hautes Études, Paris.

pur, did not appear, however, until 1944 and was the only collection of Sumerian literary texts published in the entire 1941–1950 decade.

The situation improved considerably in the course of the following decade. In 1952 my *Enmerkar and the Lord of Aratts*[14] appeared, and in 1959 Edmond Gordon published the groundbreaking, fundamental volume *Sumerian Proverbs;*[15] both these works contained copies and photographs of quite a number of tablets and fragments from the Nippur collection of the University Museum and the Museum of the Ancient Orient. In 1957, J. J. A. van Dijk published the second volume of *Tabulae Cuneiformes a F. M. Th. de Liagre Böhl Collectae,* which included seven important Sumerian literary pieces. But the most impressive contribution of the decade came in 1959, with the publication of *CT* 42, a volume containing H. H. Figulla's copies of forty-six Sumerian tablets from the British Museum.[16] This publication was doubly welcome to cuneiformists: it marked the revival, under the far-sighted sponsorship of the then Keeper of the Western Asiatic section of the British Museum, Richard Barnett, and his associate, Edmond Sollberger, of the *CT* publications that had lapsed for a quarter of a century, and it gave evidence of the unsuspected existence in the British Museum of a large number of Sumerian literary documents.

The decade that followed, that of the years of 1961–1970, was

14. This was published as a monograph of the University Museum. A revised and improved edition of this epic tale has been prepared by Sol Cohen as a dissertation in the Department of Oriental Studies of the University of Pennsylvania (1973).

15. This, too, was published as a monograph of the University Museum. Gordon followed up this study with several additional articles on Mesopotamian proverbs, based primarily on tablets and fragments from the Nippur collections of the University Museum and the Museum of the Ancient Orient.

16. For a detailed summary of the contents of these tablets, see my review article in the *Journal of Cuneiform Studies*, vol. 18 (1964), pp. 35–48, and for the collation of the texts, see ibid., vol. 23 (1970), pp. 10–16.

more productive than any of its predecessors; it witnessed the publication of more than a thousand pieces, mostly fragments to be sure, that brought to light numerous hitherto unknown literary works and helped to restore many fragmentary and unintelligible compositions. Thus in 1961 and 1967 there appeared Bernhardt and Kramer's *Sumerische Literarische Texte aus Nippur*, with copies of more than a hundred tablets and fragments from the Hilprecht Sammlung of the Friedrich-Schiller Universität, Jena.[17] In 1963 and 1966 appeared the first two parts of volume 6 of *Ur Excavation Texts*, with Cyril Gadd's copies of close to four hundred tablets and fragments excavated at Ur by the joint British Museum-University Museum Expedition conducted by Leonard Woolley in the years 1923–1934. And the last year of the decade, 1969, saw the publication of volume 1 of *Istanbul Arkeoloji Müzelerinde Bulunan Edibi Tabletler ve Parcalari* (Sumerian Literary Tablets and Fragments in the Archeological Museums of Istanbul), with copies of some six hundred pieces prepared by Muazzez Cig and Hatice Kizilyay, two Turkish ladies who had charge of the Istanbul tablet collection and who have contributed significantly to cuneiform research over the years.

As for the present decade, 1971–1979, it might turn out to be even more productive than its predecessor. To begin with, volume 2 of *Istanbul Arkeoloji Müzelerinde Bulunan Edebi Tabletler ve Parcalari*, consisting of my copies of over one hundred and seventy pieces, was published in 1976 by Türk Tarih Kurumu (the Turkish Historical Commission).[18] In the same year appeared volume 5 of

17. The copies were prepared with my help by Dr. Inez Bernhardt, who was in charge of the Hilprecht Sammlung at the time. Dr. Bernhardt, however, is no Sumerologist, and though she had a sharp eye and good hand for copying, her autographs contained quite a number of errors. These have now been corrected by Claus Wilcke's helpful collations published as part 4 of volume 65 of the *Abhandlungen der Sächischen Akademie der Wissenschaften zu Leipzig* (1976).

18. There are still about two hundred Sumerian literary pieces, mostly small fragments, in the Istanbul museum, and it is hoped that these will be copied by some Turkish scholar in the not too distant future.

the *Oxford Edition of Cuneiform Texts*, consisting of Oliver Gurney's superb copies of close to fifty tablets and fragments in the Ashmolean Museum, together with my transliterations and translations of several of the more important documents. In the British Museum, one of my former students, Aaron Shaffer, has copied close to four hundred small fragments from the above-mentioned Woolley excavations at Ur, and these will be published in the near future. In the University Museum, one of its research associates, Jane Heimerdinger, is about to complete the copying of more than five hundred small fragments from the 1948–1952 excavations of the joint Oriental Institute-University Museum expeditions to Nippur. The two American institutions that still have a number of unpublished Sumerian literary pieces are the University Museum and Yale University, and these are in the process of being copied and edited by their two curators, Åke Sjöberg and William Hallo, and by a number of younger cuneiformists under their supervision.

So much for the publication of the textual source material. As for the restoration, translation, and interpretation of the individual compositions represented by it, these may be said to have begun seriously and fruitfully in the 1930s and to have continued to make no little headway to the present day.[19] As a result of the labors of numerous scholars over the past four decades, the nature and content of the Sumerian literary repertoire can now be itemized *grosso modo* as follows: twenty myths, nine epic tales, over two hundred hymnal compositions of diverse length and genre including a considerable number of chants and dirges revolving about the Dumuzi-Inanna cult: a score or so of liturgical lamentations; a

---

19. The interested student can follow the progress of these Sumerological contributions over the years in the Assyriological bibliographical sections of *Orientalia* and the *Archiv für Orientforschung;* in R. Borger's *Handbuch der Keilschriftliteratur* (1967); in the list of Adam Falkenstein's books, articles, and reviews itemized in the *Heidelberger Studien zum Alten Orient* (1967); in the list of Thorkild Jacobsen's Sumerological contributions in *Towards the Image of Tammuz* (1970); and in the list of my books and articles in the *Kramer Anniversary Volume* (vol. 26 of *Alter Orient und Altes Testament*, 1976).

dozen disputations and school essays; and another dozen or so collections of proverbs and precepts.[20] All in all, it is not unreasonable to conclude that this immense literary stock consisting of close to thirty thousand lines of text, mostly in poetic form, provides a fairly representative cross-section of the literary repertoire current in Sumer in the Old Babylonian period, although some unexpected genres may still turn up.

Nevertheless, *a priori*, it can be surmised that the Sumerian literary material excavated to date is but a fraction of that which existed in Sumer, and that many a composition is still lying buried in its tells and ruins. Thus, there are quite a number of unidentifiable compositions of which we have at present only meager, fragmentary extracts. The numerous epithets by which the more important deities are designated imply the existence of at least some tales relating their origin, none of which has been recovered to date. Here and there in the available documents there are hints of

20. A detailed analysis of the nature and contents of the Sumerian literary works can be found in chapter 5 of my *The Sumerians; Their History, Culture and Character* (1963). Translations of quite a number of the compositions can be found in Adam Falkenstein's contribution to *Sumerische und Akkadische Hymnen und Gebete* (1953); in W. Römer's *Sumerische Königshymnen der Isin Zeit* (1965); in my contributions to *Ancient Near Eastern Texts* (3rd ed., 1969, James Pritchard, ed.); in Åke Sjöberg's *The Collection of Temple Hymns* (1969); and in G. Castellino's *Two Shulgi Hymns* (1972). Moreover, in the past fifteen years, quite a number of valuable doctoral dissertations consisting of editions of one or more of the Sumerian literary works have been prepared in various universities, especially in the University Museum of the University of Pennsylvania (first under my sponsorship and later under the sponsorship of my successor Åke Sjöberg); in the Oriental Institute of the University of Chicago (under the sponsorship of Miguel Civil); in the Babylonian Collection of the Yale University (under the sponsorship of William Hallo); and in the Assyriological Institute of the University of Munich (under the sponsorship of D. O. Edzard). A panoramic overview of the formal aspects of Sumerian literature has been published recently by Claus Wilcke in *Sumerological Studies in Honor of Thorkild Jacobsen* (1975). A comprehensive catalogue of almost all known Sumerian literary works, together with a list of the tablets and fragments, published and unpublished, that belong to each, has been prepared by Miguel Civil of the Oriental Institute of the University of Chicago, formerly my assistant in the University Museum—its publication in the near future will mark a milestone in the ongoing process of the recovery and restoration of the Sumerian *belles lettres*.

as yet altogether unknown myths, such as the avenging of Enlil by one of the lesser gods, or Enki's struggle with the *kur* and his elevation to the kingship of the *Abzu*. Most important of all is the evidence derived from the Old Babylonian literary catalogues prepared by the ancient scribes themselves. Until very recently there were known six Old Babylonian catalogues that among them listed the incipits of over one hundred and fifty Sumerian literary compositions of diverse genres, but the texts of only about sixty of these have been recovered wholly or in part. In 1975 I published, in a Festschrift honoring the eminent Finnish cuneiformist, Armas Salonen, two hitherto unknown Old Babylonian catalogues in the British Museum that were first identified by Edmond Sollberger, and these provided the titles of over one hundred *irshemma* compositions, of which only some ten have been recovered to date. It is obvious therefore that many, if not most, of the Sumerian literary works are still buried underground awaiting the lucky spade of the future excavator.

One rather unexpected, but most fruitful source for the recovery and restoration of some of the Sumerian literary documents is the vast tablet collection of the British Museum. As already noted here, it was the British Museum that virtually launched Sumerian literature on the modern scholarly scene with the publication of volume 4 of the series *Inscriptions of Western Asia* in 1875 and *CT* 15 in 1902. But then it seems to have dried up, as it were, as far as Sumerian literature was concerned—for more than half a century, the only Sumerian literary pieces published by the museum were ten tablets copied by the late C. J. Gadd in *CT* 36, which appeared in 1923. Worse yet, in 1939, following the appearance of *CT* 41, the British Museum suspended publication of the series for more than a quarter of a century, and thus created a vacuum in cuneiform research that was deeply felt and deplored by all the students of the Ancient Near East.

In 1959, under the farsighted sponsorship of Richard Barnett, then Keeper of the Western Asiatic Section, the *CT* series was revived, and to the very pleasant surprise of cuneiformists the world over the very first volume published, *CT* 42, was devoted entirely to Sumerian literature—it contained copies of more than forty Sumerian literary tablets and fragments autographed by one of its eminent researchers, H. H. Figulla, a refugee from Nazi Germany. And this was but the first intimation that the tablet collection of the museum, much of which was still uncatalogued and unstudied, was by no means exhausted as far as Sumerian literature was concerned. In the late 1960s, Edmond Sollberger, the present Keeper of the Western Asiatic Section and one of the world's leading Sumerologists, identified more than fifty Sumerian literary tablets (in the course of examining the tablet-packed cupboards for cataloguing purposes), some of which were inscribed with hitherto totally unknown Sumerian literary compositions. The examination and cataloguing of the vast museum tablet collection are now going on apace, and there is hope that many more Sumerian literary tablets, or at least fragments of tablets, will be recovered and identified in the process.

For close to ten years now, I have been privileged to spend the better part of my summers in the Students' Room of the British Museum for the purpose of studying and cataloguing the contents of the Sumerian literary tablets and fragments excavated, as it were, from the museum cupboards. Altogether I have now examined more than one hundred and fifty of these literary pieces and have come to realize that they range over the entire gamut of the Sumerian literary repertoire: myths, epic tales, hymns, laments, liturgies, "Sacred Marriage" chants, as well as a diversified group of "wisdom" compositions. Some are extracts from compositions long known; others are small fragments that often help to fill in the breaks and gaps in texts already published. But not a few of the tablets are inscribed with compositions hitherto altogether unknown.

Two of these are the precious *irshemma* catalogues mentioned earlier that were published in the Salonen Festschrift. Three are small catalogues inscribed with titles of compositions belonging to a hymnal genre known as *balag*, [21] which I plan to publish in the near future. One fairly well preserved tablet is inscribed with a very unusual myth revolving about the birth of the *elpetu*-plant.[22] Quite a number of pieces are inscribed with compositions revolving about the most complex and fascinating of all Sumerian deities, the goddess Inanna.[23]

Finally, there is a very well-preserved tablet whose contents I have prepared for publication in a memorial volume now in press that is dedicated to the late J. J. Finkelstein, one of my former students.[24] I shall conclude this section with a sketch and translation of its contents.

The tablet, catalogued as BM 24975, is inscribed with an elegy, or funeral chant, lamenting the death of a courier who met his cruel fate in the performance of some mission for a maid, not further identified in the text, who was his dearly beloved. The composition is in the form of a playlet featuring two speakers, the "maid" and an unnamed friend. It begins with an address by the friend consisting of nineteen lines in which he exhorts the "maid" to prepare herself for the imminent arrival of her beloved courier and then proceeds to apprize her in oblique, allusive, simile-laden language of his violent death in a distant land, and the return of his corpse over mountains and rivers to her and to the place from which he had started on his disastrous mission.

The response of the "maid" constitutes the remainder of the composition. If I understand it correctly, it consists of two sections.

---

21. The word *balag* probably means "harp," and it may be assumed that the *balag* chants were accompanied by that musical instrument; a detailed study of the *balag* genre was prepared in 1974 by Mark Cohen as a doctoral dissertation in the University Museum.

22. See pp. 30–36 of this volume.

23. A sketch of the contents of five of these can be found on pp. 88–96 of this volume.

24. Before sending the manuscript to press, I sent it to my Harvard colleague Thorkild Jacobsen, and I am indebted to him for a number of valuable suggestions.

In the first she itemizes all the "great things" she will provide for her courier, presumably as cult offerings to his ghost: cakes, fruits of the field, roasted barley, dates, beer, grapes on the vine, apples and figs, honey and wine, hot and cold water, rein and whip, a clean garment, fine oil, a chair, footstool and bed, cream and milk. The second section begins with the "maid's" melancholy portrayal of the dead courier upon his arrival: he is unable to walk, see, or speak. She then continues with a description of the ritual she performs immediately upon the arrival of the corpse, and concludes with the bitter realization that her smitten courier lies dead and that his spirit, now that it has been ritually liberated from his body, has departed from her house. Here is the chant as composed by the ancient elegist:

"Your courier is approaching—prepare yourself,
Oh Maid, your courier is approaching—prepare yourself,
Your dear courier is approaching—prepare yourself.

Oh, the courier! Oh, the courier!
5 Your courier, he of the far-away place,
Your courier of distant fields, of alien roads,
Your swallow that will not come forth unto distant days,
Your dragonfly of the rising waters, adrift on the river,
Your mist drifting over the mountain ranges,
10 Your river-covering mountain-grass floating on the river,
Your ibex traversing the mountains,
Your courier carried off by the head-winds,
Your courier overwhelmed by the head-winds, by the storm,
Your courier, he of evil omen,
15 Your courier, he of weeping eyes,
Your courier, he of grievous heart,
Your courier, he whose bones have been devoured by the high
    flood,

Obverse of BM 24975, a Sumerian literary tablet inscribed with a hitherto unknown elegy, lamenting the death of a courier who met his cruel fate in the performance of a mission for his beloved. With the permission of the Trustees of the British Museum.

Your floating courier, he whose head is suspended on the high
    flood,
Your courier, he who has been struck in his broad chest."

20   "After my courier has come, I will do great things for him:
     I will offer him cakes and herbs of the grove,
     I will provide him with the fruits of the field,
     I will provide him with roasted barley and dates,
     I will provide him with bitter-sweet beer,
25   I will provide him with grapes on the vine,
     I will provide him with apples of the wide earth,
     I will provide him with figs of the wide earth,
     I will provide him with the choicest fruit of the fig tree,
     I will provide him with dates on their cluster,
30   I will provide him with honey and wine from the orchard.

After my courier has come, I will provide great things for him:
     I will provide him with hot water and cold water,
     I will provide him with rein and whip,
     I will provide him with a clean garment and fine oil,
35   I will provide him with a chair and a footstool,
     I will provide him with a verdant bed,
     I will provide him with cream and milk from stall and fold.

My courier—he has come but walks not, he has come but
    walks not,
He has eyes but he cannot see me,
40   He has a mouth but he cannot converse with me.

My courier has come—approach! He has indeed
    come—approach!
I have cast down bread, wiped him clean with it,
From a drinking cup that has not been contaminated,
From a bowl that has not been defiled,

45　I poured water, and the earth where the water was poured, drank
　　　it up.
With my fine oil I anointed the wall for him,
With my new garment I clothed his chair,
The spirit has entered, the spirit has departed,
My courier was struck down on the mountain, in the heart of
　　　the mountain—he is dead."

So much for the past labors and future hopes for the recovery and
restoration of the Sumerian literary documents. As noted earlier,
the literary repertoire of the Sumerians included quite a variety of
genres, one of which consisted of their myths, that is, narrative
tales in poetic form in which the gods were the principal protagonists. Some of these concern creation, and the next chapter
will be devoted to a sketch of the various aspects of the divine
creation process as evidenced in these mythological tales and in
other relevant cuneiform documents.

II

Creation: What the Gods Have Wrought and How

For this chapter I have gone through the available Sumerian literature and have excerpted the passages that relate to the creation of the universe and its organization, the birth of the gods, and the creation of man, in an effort to search out the underlying cosmogonic ideas and cosmological concepts. This was no simple smooth-sailing exercise. To be sure, there is good reason to surmise that the creation of the universe and related matters were themes that interested deeply the Sumerian theologians, mythographers, and poets, and that they often theorized and argued about them. Unfortunately for us, the Sumerian men of letters did not devise a written literary tool for the systematic, logical formulation of their relevant views and credos—they wrote no metaphysical tracts and philosophical treatises that would make it possible for us to understand and evaluate the reasoning underlying their cosmogonic hypotheses and cosmological beliefs. What little we do know about these themes must be ferreted out passage by passage and line by line from the myths, epics, disputations, and now and then even from drab, arid, lexical texts.[1]

As of today the most significant passage for the quest for Sumerian cosmogonic ideas is the twenty-six line passage that serves as a

1. For fuller details, see my *Sumerian Mythology* (1969), pp. 30–95, and my review of *The Intellectual Adventures of Ancient Man* (Henri Frankfurt, ed.) in the *Journal of Cuneiform Studies*, vol. 2 (1948), pp. 37–70.

proem to an epic tale commonly designated as "Gilgamesh, Enkidu, and the Nether World."[2] Before reading and analyzing this passage, however, let me digress for a moment to explain and clarify a stylistic feature that characterizes the Sumerian literary style, to wit, that the most significant part of a sentence, passage, or even of an entire composition is usually placed at the end of the sentence, passage, or composition. Thus, in the case of the tale "Gilgamesh, Enkidu, and the Nether World," the poet who composed it was not interested so much in Gilgamesh and his heroic deeds as in depicting the fate of the dead in the dark, dreaded world to which they had descended after their demise:[3] how, for example, fared there the man who had but one son as contrasted with the man who had seven sons; how fared the woman who bore no children, the dead who had no one to tend to his ghost, the man who was killed in battle, the unfortunate who was burned alive, and so on. To do this, however, to reveal the lot of the dead in the mysterious Nether World, the poet found it necessary to utilize a device well known in the ancient literary world—having the ghost of some prominent dead man brought up from the lower regions to tell it "as it is" to a living individual who was his friend and intimate; this motif was utilized, for example, by the author of the Book of Samuel, who had Saul bring up Samuel from the dead, and by the author of the Iliad, who had Achilles raise up the ghost of Patroclus. In our case, the poet had the ghost of Enkidu, Gilgamesh's faithful servant and companion, brought up from the Nether World in order to inform his master, and incidentally the readers or listeners, of the melancholy fate of some of its denizens.

First, however, the poet felt compelled to explain the presence of Enkidu in the Nether World, that is, how he got there and why. In

2. For a preliminary translation of this epic tale, see *The Sumerians*, pp. 197–205; a definitive edition of the text was prepared as part of a dissertation in the University Museum by Aaron Shaffer in 1967.

3. For the rather confused and even contradictory Sumerian notions about the Nether World, see *Iraq*, vol. 22 (1960), pp. 59–68.

the passage preceding the raising of Enkidu's ghost, therefore, the poet informs us that Enkidu had descended to the world below fearlessly and of his own volition in order to retrieve for Gilgamesh two objects precious to his master, the *pukku* and *mekku*.[4] While there he had broken some of its tabus and as a consequence the Nether World "held him fast," that is, he was as good as dead, though he had not died as other men do.

But how did Gilgamesh's *pukku* and *mekku* get into the Nether World, and how did Gilgamesh obtain them in the first place? This is told in a preceding long narrative section that runs as follows: One day, the goddess Inanna, walking along the bank of the Euphrates, noticed a lone *huluppu*-tree,[5] whose roots and crown had been plucked and torn by the violent South Wind, floating in the river. Fearfully, she took the tree out of the water and brought it to her city Erech. There she tended it carefully in the hope of seeing it grow big and strong so that she could make a throne and a couch for herself from its wood. Years passed. The tree did mature, but the goddess dared not come near it, for

In its roots the snake who knows no charm had set up its nest,
In its crown the *Imdugud*-bird[6] had placed its young,
In its midst Lilith,[7] the maid, had built her house.

Bitterly disappointed, the weeping Inanna turned to her brother the sun-god Utu for help, but her plea was rejected. She then turned

4. The meaning of these two words that are probably Akkadian loan-words from the Sumerian is still uncertain. The most reasonable suggestion to date is that they are to be rendered "drum" and "drumstick."

5. The *huluppu* tree has been very tentatively identified as the willow.

6. The word *Imdugud* is now read by some scholars as *Anzu*, but this is not quite certain, and for the present I prefer the long-accepted reading *Imdugud*. The Imdugud-bird plays a considerable role in Sumerian mythology, but it is portrayed quite differently in the various episodes in which it takes part, and its symbolic, mythopoeic character is by no means clear; see for the present Claus Wilcke's *Das Lugalbanda Epos* (1969), pp. 61–64.

7. Lilith is actually a loan-word that goes back to the Sumerian *lil*, which has a semantic range corresponding to the Hebrew *ruach*, "wind," "spirit," "demon."

22

for help to the hero Gilgamesh, and he decided to stand by her. He donned his armor, weighing fifty *minas*,[8] took up his huge axe, and slew the snake at the base of the tree. This so terrified the *Imdugud*-bird that it fled with its young to the distant mountains, while Lilith tore down her house in the middle of the tree and fled to her desolate haunts. Gilgamesh then gave the tree to the goddess for her holy throne and bed, while from its roots he fashioned a *pukku* and from its crown he fashioned a *mekku*. Unhappily he used these objects to oppress in some way the citizens of Erech, particularly, it seems, by summoning the young men to war and thus making widows of their wives. As the poet puts it, it was "because of the cries of the young maidens" that the *pukku* and *mekku* fell into the Nether World. Gilgamesh tried desperately to retrieve them, but failed, and when Enkidu saw his master's distress, he unhesitatingly volunteered to descend to the world below to bring them up, and lost his life in the process.

It is the prologue to the events narrated in this section of the poem that includes the revealing creation passage, which reads as follows:

In primeval days, in distant primeval days,
In primeval nights, in far-off primeval nights,
In primeval years, in distant primeval years —
In ancient days when everything vital had been brought into
    existence,
5 In ancient days when everything vital had been nurtured,
When bread had been tasted in the shrines of the land [Sumer],
When bread had been baked in the ovens of the land —
When heaven had been moved away from the earth,
When earth had been separated from heaven,
10 When the name of man had been fixed —
When An had carried off heaven,
When Enlil had carried off earth,

8. A *mina* is roughly equal to a pound.

When Ereshkigal had been carried off into the *kur* as its prize—
When he had set sail, when he had set sail,
15 When the Father had set sail for the *kur*,
When Enki had set sail for the *kur*,
Against the king it hurled the little ones,
Against Enki it hurled the big ones,
Its little ones being "stones of the hand,"
20 Its big ones being stones that "make reeds dance,"
They overwhelm the keel of Enki's boat like onrushing turtles,
Against the king, the waters at the bow of the boat
Devour like a wolf,
Against Enki, the waters at the rear of the boat
25 Strike dead like a lion—
In those days, a lone tree, a lone *huluppu*-tree, a lone tree
Planted on the bank of the holy Euphrates (etc.)

The poet who composed this tale—as is clear from the lines "When heaven had been moved away from earth," "When earth had been moved away from heaven," "When An had carried off heaven," "When Enlil had carried off earth"—conceived of a primeval time when a united heaven and earth had been sundered from each other, and following this separation it was the heaven-god An who carried off heaven as his domain, while the air-god Enlil carried off the earth as his realm. Below the earth, and surrounding it on all sides, however, was another realm of the universe known as *kur*, of which the Nether World was part—a dark, murky, demon-infested region[9] whose ruler tried to interfere in some way with the creative process. It was the water-god Enki who ventured forth in his boat to vanquish this violent, tempestu-

9. This is only one facet of the meaning of the word *kur*, which is written with a sign that goes back to a pictograph for "mountain." Its more original meaning, therefore, was probably "mountain" or "highland," and since the highlands to the north and east of Sumer were inhabited by peoples who were often at war with Sumer, it came to mean "inimical land"; see especially the myth "The Deeds and Exploits of Ninurta," whose contents are sketched in pp. 37–39 of this volume.

ous, stone-flinging *kur*.[10] Unfortunately the author leaves us stranded at this point and does not tell us who won the battle, but there is little doubt that Enki was the victor, since he was designated at times as *en-kur*, "Lord Kur," a name that must have originally belonged to the toppled ruler of the *kur*.

One very important detail relating to the creation of the universe is omitted by our poet: the identity of the deity who separated heaven from earth. For this bit of significant information we must turn to the introductory passage of another composition, a myth in which the gods celebrate the creation of the pickaxe.[11] To us the lowly pickaxe may not stand out as an implement worthy of special divine attention. But to the Sumerians, the pickaxe was the most useful technological tool at their disposal and was esteemed even more than the plow. Thus, in a composition consisting primarily of a disputation between the plow and pickaxe, it is the latter that is adjudged the victor because of the service it renders mankind in such essential activities as irrigation, drainage, and cultivation of the soil; because of its contribution to the welfare and earning capacity of the working class, particularly construction workers, boatmen, and gardeners; because it is so concerned about the well-being of road-workers that it helps to construct special towers where they can refresh themselves and fill their water-skins.[12]

To return to the myth celebrating the pickaxe and its introductory passage relating to the separation of heaven and earth:

10. The Sumerian word usually written with a sign that is generally read *Engur* (rather than *Enkur*) came to signify the vast, tempestuous, monster-infested sea. A word that is at times synonymous with *Engur* is *Abzu*, and the watery shrine of Enki, the god in charge of seas and rivers, is sometimes designated as *Abzu* and sometimes *E-Engur-ra*, "Sea-House."

11. For a sketch of this myth, see *Sumerian Mythology*, pp. 51–53.

12. This disputation has been edited by Miguel Civil as a dissertation in the École Pratique des Hautes Études (Paris); an English translation based on this dissertation can be found in my article "Sumerian Culture and Society: The Cuneiform Documents and Their Anthropological Significance" that appeared in 1965 in the Addison-Wesley *Modular Publications in Anthropology*.

The Lord made sure to bring forth whatever is vital,
The Lord whose decisions are unalterable,
Enlil, who brings up the seed of the land from the earth,
Made great haste to move away heaven from earth,
Made great haste to move away earth from heaven.

Not altogether unexpectedly, therefore, we learn that it was the air-god Enlil, the god originally in charge of the atmosphere, who separated Father Heaven from Mother Earth.

The Sumerian credo that in most ancient primeval days heaven and earth were united, and had to be separated before plants, animals, and man could come into existence, was current to some extent all through the millennia of Mesopotamian history. To be sure, the poems including the extracts just cited have thus far been found inscribed on tablets dating from the first half of the second millennium B.C., but there is good reason to surmise that these were modified redactions of earlier tablets. One such tablet that has found its way into the Yale Babylonian Collection has just been published by the Dutch cuneiformist J. J. Van Dijk. It is a very small tablet that can be dated by its script to the last century of the third millennium B.C., and its text is poorly preserved and rather obscure. But several lines are reasonably clear and these speak of the three realms of the universe, heaven, earth, and *kur*; of a time when the earth was dark, arid, and barren, since heaven and earth were still unseparated; of a time when the moon had not yet been created and blackness was everywhere, when the *me*, the universal laws, of the air-god Enlil did not yet function and the gods of heaven and earth did not yet exist.

To return now to the first two creation passages cited earlier and to the credo that after the earth (*ki* in Sumerian) had been separated from heaven (*an* in Sumerian), it was An (Father Heaven) who carried off heaven (that is, *an*) while it was their son, the air-god Enlil, who carried off the earth (that is, *ki*). On closer examination this view seems rather puzzling and anomalous, since one might

26

reasonably have expected that just as it was An (Father Heaven) who carried off heaven (*an*), it was Ki (Mother Earth) who carried off the earth (*ki*). For some reason or other, one is forced to conclude, the role of the goddess Ki, Mother Earth, had been usurped by the male deity Enlil. This brings us to the not altogether irrelevant subject of the status of woman in Sumerian sociejty, and how this might help explain the downgrading of Ki in the divine hierarchy.

In the days of the long-known social reformer Urukagina, that is, in the twenty-fourth century B.C., there is evidence to demonstrate that the Sumerian woman was man's equal, socially and economically, at least among the upper classes. There is even one woman, Enheduanna by name, a princess to be sure, who was not only the spiritual head of one of Sumer's largest and most important temples, but also a poet and author of renown. In the centuries that followed, however, the status of woman in Sumerian society deteriorated considerably, although even then she could own property and on occasion buy and sell without consulting her husband.[13]

But what is of interest to us here is the fact that it was not only on the human plane that women lost some of their rights and prerogatives in the course of the centuries, but that it happened also on the divine plane. Some of the female deities that had held top rank in the Sumerian pantheon were gradually forced down the hierarchical ladder by the male theologians who may have manipulated the order of the deities in accordance with their chauvinistic predilictions. And, as can be demonstrated from texts relating to the arrangement of leading deities of the Sumerian pantheon, one of the sharpest declines was suffered by none other than Ki, Mother Earth, the goddess who was the twin of An, Father Heaven. For as Mother Earth, whose sexual union with Father Heaven ushered in the birth of the gods unto their generations, she should have been

13. For fuller details, see my "The Sumerian Woman: Wife, Mother, Priestess, Goddess" in *The Legacy of Sumer* (Denise Schmandt-Besserat, ed., 1976).

the deity in charge of the earth and ranked second only to Father Heaven, if not his equal. But the theologians, apparently unhappy with a female deity as the ruler of so all-important a cosmic realm as the earth, had the power taken away from her and transferred to her son, the air-god Enlil who, as the poets put it, "carried off the earth" after it had been separated from heaven. As if this were not enough, they also deprived her of the name Ki, "Earth," since it no longer accorded with her reduced status. Instead they called her by one of several epithets, especially by the compound word *nin-hursag*, "Queen of the Mountain." As for her rank in the pantheon, Ki, now designated Ninhursag, was demoted from second to third place, and later even further down to fourth, third place going to the male deity Enki, whose name actually contains the element *ki* reminiscent of the goddess's original name.

Now that she had been deprived of much of her power as well as her name and was but a weak reflection of her former self, Ki could no longer be worshipped and adored as the mother of Enlil, the god who gradually became the leading deity of the Sumerian pantheon. Instead she was conceived by the theologians as Enlil's "big sister," as we first learn from an archaic text on a clay cylinder, excavated by the University of Pennsylvania almost a century ago, that probably dates back to the twenty-fourth century B.C. Much of its contents is still unintelligible, but its introductory lines depict the sexual union of Enlil and his "big sister" Ninhursag probably in Enlil's Nippur shrine, a union that, according to the poet, was accompanied by storms, lightning, and thunder.

Nor is the goddess Ki the only female deity who suffered demotion at the hands of the theologians. If we think back to the creation passages cited earlier, which speak of the separation of heaven and earth, it will be noted that they imply a belief in the primeval existence of a united heaven and earth, as well as of the deities An, "Heaven," and Ki, "Earth." But they say nothing about the parentage of the couple, nor how heaven and earth were brought into existence in the first place. For this information we must turn, not to a literary document, but to a lexical text consisting of a list of deities, according to which the sea-goddess Nammu was "the mother who gave birth to heaven and earth." This same goddess Nammu, moreover, is described in a Sumerian myth concerned with the creation of man as "the mother who gave birth to all the gods." By all genealogical rights, therefore, had the theologians played it fair, she should have had top billing in the pantheon. But in the god-lists where the deities are arranged in hierarchical order she is rarely mentioned, and never at the head of the list. Moreover, her vast powers as goddess of the sea were turned over to the male deity Enki, who was then designated by the theologians as the son of Nammu, in an apparent attempt to mitigate and justify this bit of priestly piracy. Even so, the king who founded the Third Dynasty of Ur and ushered in a political and cultural Sumerian renaissance toward the close of the third millennium B.C. chose as his royal name *ur-(dingir) nammu*, "Servant of the goddess Nammu," which indicates that the goddess was still worshipped and adored by the mighty of the land.

Not all mythographers believed that the separation of heaven and earth was a *sine qua non* for their creative acts. Thus, according to one poet, the birth of Tree and Reed (personified) resulted directly and immediately from the sexual union of Heaven and Earth, as is evidenced by the introductory lines of the "Disputation between Tree and Reed," in which the poet depicts in concrete, picturesque, metaphorical language the birth of these two personified forms of vegetation:

The great Earth-crust was resplendent, its surface was
    jewel-green,
The wide Earth—its surface was covered with precious metals
    and lapis lazuli,
It was adorned with diorite, *nir*-stone, carnelian, and antimony,
The Earth was arrayed luxuriantly in plants and herbs, its
    presence was majestic,

5 The holy Earth, the pure Earth, beautified herself for holy
      Heaven,
   Heaven, the noble god, inserted his sex into the wide Earth,
   Let flow the semen of the heroes, Trees and Reed, into her
      womb,
   The Earthly Orb, the trusty cow, was impregnated with the good
      semen of Heaven.[14]

Another example of the birth of vegetation as a direct result of
the sexual union of Heaven and Earth is provided by a tablet in the
British Museum that I recently copied and am in the process of
preparing for publication. This tablet is inscribed with a very
unusual mythological poem that revolves about the birth and
misdeeds of a reedy plant known as *numun*, generally taken to be a
reed growing especially alongside canals. Only about two-thirds of
the poem, originally about ninety lines in length, is preserved.
Moreover, though the reading and rendering of most of the individual words and phrases are reasonably assured, their connota-
tions and implications are obscure, and the interrelationship of the
separate passages is quite uncertain—so much so that when I first
announced the contents of the tablet in a paper read before the
Rencontre Assyriologique Internationale in Göttingen in 1974, I
felt compelled to entitle it "BM 120011: A Myth in Need of a
Grotefend," Grotefend being the brilliant Göttingen scholar who
was one of the very first cuneiform decipherers. Before and during
the Rencontre I invited some of my Sumerological colleagues to
study the text and to try to come up with a translation and interpretation. Several of them did make a number of helpful
suggestions, but on the whole the contents of the myth remain
perplexing, problematical, and enigmatic. Here, now, to the best
of my understanding, is a provisional sketch of the plot of the myth.
   After a devastating Flood had been sent down to earth as a

14. This translation is based on an as yet unpublished edition of the text prepared
by Miguel Civil.

punishment against man because of his addiction to mutual confrontation and defiance as well as to carnal lust,[15] Father Heaven once again impregnated Mother Earth, who then gave birth to the plants, including the *numun*-plant that set afire everything in its path. This *numun*-plant, moreover, was a source of back-breaking labor to all who had escaped destruction by the Flood: to the old people, to the chief temple-choristers, and to whomever else had been spared by the Deluge. It could not be made into bundles, or even budged or loosened from its spot. If it was made into a reed hut, it swayed and tottered. Once it ignited a fire, the blaze was uncontrollable and spread far and wide. It hopped about among the bitter waters that were its home-base, as it were, eager to set fires.

But one day this *numun*-plant miscalculated and went too far with its mischievous talents—it tried to set afire the temple of the goddess Inanna known as Eanna, "the House of Heaven," whereupon it was bound and fettered. When it complained about this mistreatment, the goddess seized a raven and set it on top of the *numun*-plant. But, in some way not stated in the text, this action of the goddess seemed to offend the shepherd (the demigod Dumuzi), who proceeded to abandon Inanna's sheep in their reed enclosures.

Dumuzi's defiance so enraged Inanna that she sent another devastating Flood, directed this time primarily against the shepherd and his stalls and sheepfolds. Its floodwaters and fierce winds also overwhelmed the rivers and marshes, and alongside the Tigris and Euphrates there grew nothing but tall grass. There then follows a very fragmentary passage of ten lines whose contents are altogether uncertain—to judge from the text that follows, something may have happened to soothe the anger of the goddess. In any case when

15. This is a version of the Flood myth quite unlike that known hitherto from cuneiform sources (see *Sumerian Mythology*, pp. 97–99, and Expedition 9/4 [1967], pp. 12–18) but reminiscent to some extent of the Flood passage near the very end of the epic tale "Enmerkar and the Lord of Aratta" (see footnote 14, Chapter 1, this volume). What is of special interest about this version of the Flood myth is that it parallels the Biblical Flood story in one very important aspect—in both cases the Flood is sent against man because of his aggressive, lustful behavior.

the text becomes legible, we learn that someone had bundled up the *numun*-plant and was guarding it for Inanna, and that sundry craftsmen were tending to her needs: the fuller provided her with clean garments, the carpenter with her weaving spindle, the potter with earthen vessels for food and drink. Whereupon the goddess raised a cry that resounded all over heaven and earth and pronounced a curse against the *numun*-plant. Unfortunately the nature of the curse must remain a mystery for the present since the remainder of the poem, approximately thirty lines of text, is completely destroyed.

Following is a tentative translation of this unique document:[16]

The old man instructed, the old man exhorted:
After the rain had poured down, after it had demolished walls,
After hailstones and firebrands had poured down,
After man had confronted man defiantly,
5 After there had been copulation—he had also copulated,
After there had been kissing—he had also kissed,
After the rain had said: "I will pour down,"
After it had said: "I will demolish walls,"
After the Flood had said: "I will sweep everything away,"
10 Heaven impregnated, Earth gave birth,
Gave birth to the *numun*-plant, also,
Earth gave birth, Heaven impregnated,
Gave birth to the *numun*-plant, also,
Its luxuriant reeds kindled fires.

16. In this translation note the following: the "de-de-defied" in line 15 attempts to render a similar partial repetition in the Sumerian; the "it" in this line refers to the *numun* plant; the translation of lines 16–18 is reasonably assured, but the connotation and implication of the passage are elusive and obscure; in line 28, the word "saying" is to be understood after "Hops about"; in lines 42, the three dots following "The" represent a Sumerian phrase that is unintelligible; lines 62 and 63 contain literary clichés known from a number of Sumerian compositions; the second part of lines 65–67 is destroyed on the tablet (hence the four dots which here, and throughout, stand for three or more broken or unintelligible words).

15   They who de-de-defied it,
      The old women who had been spared by Day,
      The old men who had been spared by Day,
      The chief temple-choristers who had been spared by Year,
      Whosoever had been spared by the Flood,
20   Were crushed by labor,
      Were crushed by labor, crouched in the dust.

      The *numun*-plant is a fire-kindler, it cannot be tied into
          bundles,
      The plant cannot be budged, the plant cannot be loosened,
      The plant cannot be loosened. When made into an enclosure,
25   It stands up one moment, lies down the next.
      Having kindled a fire, it spreads wide.
      The *numun*-plant, among the bitter waters that are its habitat,
      Hops about: "I will set, I will set fire."

      It set fire to the base of the Eanna,
30   There it was bound, there it was fettered,
      When it protested,
      Inanna seized a raven, set it over it,
      The shepherd abandoned his sheep in their enclosures
      To Inanna who had seized the raven.

35   After the rain had poured down, after it had demolished walls,
      After hailstones and firebrands had poured down,
      Against Dumuzi who had defied it,
      The rain poured down, demolished walls,
      Demolished stalls, ripped out sheepfolds,
40   Hurled vicious floodwaters into the rivers,
      Hurled vicious winds into the marshes,
      The . . . of the Tigris and Euphrates
      Made tall grass grow by the Tigris and Euphrates.

33

Obverse of BM 120011, a Sumerian literary tablet inscribed with a hitherto unknown mythological poem that revolves about the birth and misdeeds of the numun-plant. With the permission of the Trustees of the British Museum.

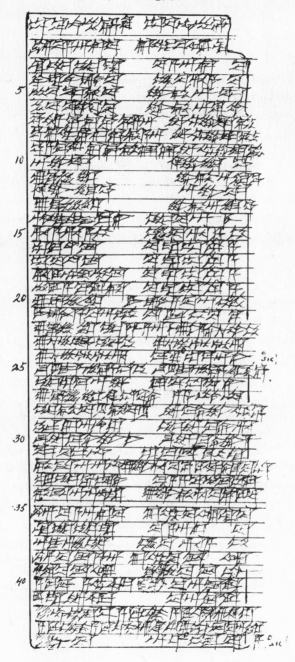

120011 obverse

Dr. Kramer's hand-copy of the obverse of BM 120011.

[Break of ten lines]

He bundled up the fire-kindling *numun*-plant,
55 Bundled up the fire-kindler, guards it for her,
For Inanna—the fuller cleansed her garments,
Inanna—the carpenter made her hold the weaving-spindle in
her hand,
Inanna—the potter kneaded cups and pitchers.
That potter gave her holy drinking-bowls. The shepherd brought
her his sheep,
60 The shepherd brought her his sheep, guards them for her,
Brought her all kinds of luxurious plants as her harvest.

She cried out to Heaven, cried out to Earth,
Her cries in their totality covered the horizon like a garment,
spread over it like a cloth,
She hurled a curse on the head of the *numun*-plant:
65 Oh numun-plant may your name be . . . . ,
You who are a plant. . . .
You who are a hateful plant. . . .
[Remainder of the tablet destroyed]

It is not always the sexual union of Heaven and Earth that is essential for the birth-giving process—there is at least one case in which the air-god Enlil is depicted as having intercourse with the mountains and inseminating them with offspring. Of this union, however, it is not verdant plants that are born, but the two personified seasons Summer and Winter, which the god planned and begot for the welfare of mankind. Or, as the poet puts it:[17]

17. The passage, consisting of the introductory lines of "The Disputation between Summer and Winter," is based on an edition of the composition prepared by Miguel Civil that is still unpublished. Note that Nunamnir (line 1) is another name for Enlil, and that the dots at end of lines 7 and 11 represent Sumerian phrases that are unintelligible.

Nunamnir [Enlil] lifted his head, brought forth the good day,
Laid plans for the universe, spread them wide over the lands,
Enlil set his foot upon the earth like a great bull.

To make the good day come forth in abundance,
5 To bring forth the good night in luxuriance,
To make grow many plants, to spread wide the grain,
To make sure of the overflow at the quays . . . . ,
To make Summer hold back the heaven's rain,
To make sure of the waters of abundance at the quays,
10 Enlil, the king of all the lands, set his mind.

He inserted his sex into the great mountains . . . .
He inseminated their womb with Summer and Winter, the
    dependable abundance of the land,
Wherever Enlil inserted his sex, there was a roar,
At the mountains he whiled away the day, rejoiced at night,
15 He pressed Summer and Winter out of them like good cream,
He made them eat pure plants like wild oxen on the mountain
    terraces,
He made them grow thick and strong in the mountain valleys.

How the mountains came into being, or at least the Zagros
ranges immediately to the east of Sumer, is the theme of a myth
which has been known in part for many decades, but which has
only recently been pieced together almost in its entirety by several
scholars from more than one hundred and fifty tablets and fragments scattered throughout museums and collections the world
over.[18] The myth may be entitled "The Deeds and Exploits of

18. The scholars who are to be credited with this achievement are the late Eugen
Bergmann, who copied many of the relevant tablets and fragments in the University
Museum under my guidance, and especially J. J. Van Dijk and his student José
Zubizaretta, who have prepared a definitive edition of the myth that is to be
published in the near future.

Ninurta," Ninurta being the bellicose god of the tempestuous South Wind who is also conceived by the mythographers as the "Farmer of Enlil," whose son he was, his mother being Enlil's "big sister" Ninhursag. The tale begins with Ninurta's violent attack against the *kur*[19] and its vicious demon the Asag, who rather surprisingly was born when Heaven inseminated Earth—the union of Heaven and Earth could thus evidently give birth to destructive forces as well as creative. After slaying the monster in the *kur*, Ninurta performs another beneficent deed with the poet depicts as follows:

There was a time when the fresh, cold water that came out of the earth never reached Sumer's fields and farms, and flowed into the desolate places of the *kur* instead. As a consequence the gods of Sumer suffered from dire famine, and had to carry "pickaxe and basket"[20] to provide for themselves the best they could. The Tigris carried no fresh water and did not overflow its banks; canals were not cleansed; dykes were not built; fields were not watered; furrows stood empty and barren. Whereupon Ninurta resolved to put an end to this catastrophic situation: he heaped up the stones of the conquered *kur* into a huge mound which closed off Sumer like a high wall, and which held back the mighty waters so that they no longer flowed into the *kur*. He then gathered all the waters that had formerly spread uselessly and wastefully over the *kur*, and poured them into the Tigris, whose overflow, in turn, watered field and farm, gardens and groves. The storehouses of Sumer were now crammed full with grain, there was great joy in the land, and all of its gods now glorified and adored their savior Ninurta.

It was then that Ninurta's mother, Ninmah, was filled with compassion for her son who lived in the far-off, hazardous *kur* that he had conquered, and went forth to pay him a congratulatory visit. Ninurta was so moved by the sight of his mother venturing all alone

19. For the meaning of *kur* in this myth, see footnote 9 of this chapter.
20. "Carrying the pickaxe and the basket" is a Sumerian stereotype for "hard labor."

into the dangerous, inimical *kur* that he named the huge mound of stones he had heaped up *hursag*, "Mountain," and named his mother *nin-hursag*, "Queen of the Mountain." In the words of the poet:

Since you, oh Woman, have come to the *kur*,
Since you, Noble Lady, because of my fame, have come to
    enemy land,
Since you feared not my terrifying battles,
I, the hero, the mound I had heaped up
5 Shall be called *hursag*, and you shall be its queen,
From now on, Nihursag is the name by which you shall be
    called—thus shall it be.
Its valleys shall be verdant with vegetation for you,
Its slopes shall produce honey and wine for you,
Shall produce for you cedar, cyprus, *zabalum*-trees, and
    boxwood on its terraces,
10 Shall be adorned with fruit for you like a garden,
The *hursag* shall provide you amply with the fragrance of the
    gods,
Shall provide you gold and silver in abundance,
Shall mine for you copper and tin, shall carry them to you as
    tribute,
The *kur* shall multiply cattle large and small for you,
15 The *hursag* shall bring forth for you the seed of all four-legged
    creatures.[21]

Etiological explanations of the creation and formation of the physical features of the cosmos, such as the *hursag*, "Mountain," in the myth just sketched, are virtually nonexistent in Sumerian literature. There are, for example, no myths explaining the creation of the moon, sun, planets, and stars, although there is some indirect evidence for the inference that the luminous bodies were

21. See lines 390–405 of the Van Dijk-Zubizaretta manuscript; note that the *zabalum*-tree in line 9 is still unidentified.

regarded as "spin-offs" of the atmosphere, since Enlil, the god of the atmosphere, was conceived as the father of the moon-god Nanna and Nanna was conceived as the father of the sun-god Utu and the Venus-goddess Inanna.[22] There is, however, a rather remarkable myth depicting the birth of the moon-god Nanna and three of his brother deities, whose presence in the Nether World seems to have troubled the mythographers; the myth is also of considerable sociological significance, since it demonstrates indirectly the Sumerian dedication to law and order—even the greatest and the mightiest had to be punished if he transgressed civilized behavior as embodied in the *me*, those laws, rules, and norms governing civilized life.

According to this rather unusual tale, Enlil forced the innocent young goddess Ninlil, who later became his respectable wife, to have intercourse with him against her will, and the gods seized him and banished him to the Nether World, despite his preeminent place in the pantheon. Ninlil, however, had become pregnant by the moon-god, and so she decided to follow her husband-to-be to the Lower Regions. Enlil repeatedly tried to elude her, but without success, so that on the way to Hades he found it necessary to impregnate her with three deities who were destined to stay in the Nether World—only Nanna, fortunately for mankind, ascended to heaven to take charge of the moon.[23]

The birth of the gods is also the theme of another remarkable myth, whose scene of action takes place in Dilmun, the Sumerian divine paradise land. The major protagonists of this myth are the water-god Enki and Enlil's "big sister" Ninhursag, who seemed to be ill-disposed toward Enki and from time to time did not hesitate to humiliate him. Ninhursag, according to the poet, had succeeded in bringing into being eight plants in Dilmun, by an intricate process involving the birth of three generations of god-

22. See *Sumerian Mythology*, pp. 41–43.
23. See ibid., pp. 43–47.

desses. But Enki, eager to taste these plants, had them plucked one by one, eating each in turn. This so enraged Ninhursag that she pronounced on him the curse of death, and Enki became sick in eight of his organs, one for each plant he had devoured. The greedy Enki would no doubt have died had not Ninhursag felt sorry for him and given birth to eight deities, each healing one of the eight of the god's sick organs.[24]

The birth of the gods is also the theme of an introductory creation passage in a composition that consists primarily of a disputation between the two sister deities Cattle and Grain.[25] The author conceives of a time when the heaven gods known as the Anunna had already been born on the "mountain of heaven and earth" but had no food to eat, nor any clothing to wear, since neither the grain-goddess Ashnan nor her sister, the cattle-goddess Lahar, had yet been created. There were indeed humans, according to this writer, but "they knew not the eating of bread," "they knew not the wearing of clothes"; they walked naked in the land, ate herbs with their mouths like sheep, and drank water out of the gullies. Then in the creation chamber of the gods known as Duku, Grain and Cattle were created, but still the Anunna-gods remained unsated until "man was given the breath of life" and Lahar and Ashnan were sent down from heaven to earth, bringing with them prosperity and abundance to the land, thus:

Lahar standing in the sheepfold,
A shepherdess fecundating the sheepfold is she,
Ashnan standing in the furrow,
A fair maid full of allure is she,

24. See my monograph *Enki and Ninhursag: A Sumerian Paradise Myth* published as *Supplementary Study No. 1* of the *Bulletin* of the American Schools of Oriental Research (1975); this is the myth which Stephen Langdon entitled "The Sumerian Epic of Paradise, the Flood, and the Fall of Man" (see footnote 10 of Chapter 1, this volume).
25. See *Sumerian Mythology*, pp. 53–54.

5   Raising a verdant head above her field,
    Walking in heaven-sent abundance.

    Lahar and Ashnan wrought wondrously,
    Brought abundance to the assembly,
    Brought the breath of life to the land,
10 Carried out the *me* of the gods.
    In the storehouse of the land goods multiplied,
    In the warehouses of the land stocks were heavy,
    Into the indigent homes pressing close to the dust,
    Stooping low they bring abundance,
15 The two of them wherever they set foot,
    Bring heavy increase to the home,
    Are meet for wherever people stand, are fitting for wherever
       people sit,
    They delight the heart of An and Enlil.

Originally, as the introduction to the Lahar-Ashnan disputation reveals, some Sumerian mythographers believed that there had existed savage, animal like humans who walked about naked and did not even know how to use their hands for eating and drinking. But then, the author tells us, "man was given the breath of life" and thus presumably lost his barbaric Neanderthal traits, and became homo sapiens, as it were, so that he could provide the gods with food and clothing. This theme of the creation of man for the purpose of providing for the needs of the gods is also found in another and more detailed myth,[26] whose contents unfortunately still remain largely obscure. According to this tale, the gods, having married and reared families, had to work very hard just to keep alive. They therefore complained to Nammu, the mother of all the gods, and she aroused her son Enki who was asleep in his watery

26. For this myth, entitled "Enki and Ninmah: The Creation of Man," see ibid., pp. 68–73; an up-to-date edition of this myth was prepared by Carlos Benito in the University Museum in 1970.

shrine, the *Abzu*, to come to the aid of the weeping gods.[27] Enki, in his wisdom, brought forth certain creatures designated in Sumerian as *sigen-sigdu*,[28] and endowed them with some of his own wisdom. He then instructed his mother Nammu to "mix the heart of the clay that is on top of the *Abzu*" so that the wise *sigen-sigdu* could nip off the clay. Nammu was then to shape this clay, while Ninmah, the goddess in charge of child-birth,[29] together with seven minor female deities helped in the intricate process of fashioning the creature destined to become the servant of the gods. The crucial lines depicting the actual appearance of man are fragmentary and obscure, but it can be assumed that he was a perfect specimen of which all concerned could well be proud.

But then the alcohol-addiction of the gods, a frequent motif in Sumerian mythology, came into play, and mankind suffered a severe setback as a consequence. At a banquet of the gods in celebration of the creation of man, Enki and Ninmah drank much beer and "their hearts became elated," that is, they became "high" and began to hurl challenges at each other. First Ninmah created six defective humans—three who were crippled in one way or another, as well as a blind man, a woman who could not give birth, and a man "who had neither phallus nor vulva in his body"—and challenged Enki to find a place for these six disadvantaged humans in society where they could function and earn their bread. Enki took up the challenge and succeeded in finding a useful position for each of the unfortunates, the first recorded example of the need and obligation to find useful work for the handicapped. To the blind man, for example, he gave the "art of song"; for the barren woman he made the harem; for the eunuch he found work in the service of the king.

27. For the goddess Nammu and her son Enki, see pp. 28–29 of this volume.
28. The meaning of this crucial word is still unknown.
29. Ninmah is another name for the mother goddess, originally probably Ki, (Mother) Earth, who also came to be known as Ninhursag; see pp. 37–39 of this volume.

Enki then turns his hand to creation and produces a creature
designated as *umul* in Sumerian—whom some scholars take to be
an "old man," whereas others hold a diametrically opposite view,
taking it to be a "new-born babe"—and challenges Ninmah to find
a place in society for him. But the goddess can do nothing with the
creature, who could not speak, nor eat, nor lie down, nor do
anything useful, and she proceeds to chide Enki for creating this
defective being who was neither dead nor alive. The remainder of
the text is fragmentary and obscure, and as of today we do not know
just what happened to the unfortunate *umul*.

While the creation of man seemed to have been an intricate,
complex, and even risky process, creation in general was no serious
problem for the gods, since the Sumerian theologians conceived
the simple and rather attractive doctrine of the creative power of the
divine word, especially the word of the leading deities of the
pantheon. According to this belief, all the deity had to do was to
draw up the plan for that which was to be created or produced, then
utter the word, and it came to be. Here for example, is a poet's
glorification of the word of Enlil:

You, lord Enlil, who are lord, god, and king,
Who are the judge and decision-maker of the universe,
Your noble word is as weighty as heaven, you know no
    opposition,
At your word, all the Anunna-gods are hushed,
5 Your word—heavenward it is a pillar, earthward it is a
    foundation-platform,
Heavenward it is a tall pillar reaching to the sky,
Earthward it is a foundation-platform that cannot be overturned.

It approaches heaven—there is overflow,
From heaven overflow rains down on earth.
10 It approaches earth—there is luxuriance,
From the earth luxuriance burgeons forth,

Your word—it is plants, your word—it is grain,
Your word is the floodwater, the life of all the lands.[30]

Enki, too, when organizing the universe, does so primarily by the word of his mouth that is authoritative and eternal, or as the god himself soliloquizes;

At my command stalls are built, sheepfolds are enclosed,
When it approaches heaven, the rain of abundance pours down
    from heaven,
When it approaches earth, there is high flood,
When it approaches the green meadow,
5 The grain-heaps and mounds are piled high at my word.[31]

As for the successful and harmonious operation of the universe "and the fullness thereof," once created, this too offered no insurmountable hurdle to the Sumerian theologians, who believed that all the essential relevant plans and laws had been drawn up in great detail at the time of creation, and that these consisted of a comprehensive assortment of powers and duties, norms and standards, rules and regulations, rights, powers, and insignia relating to the cosmic realms; to countries, cities, and temples; to the acts of gods and men, and to virtually every aspect of civilized life. The Sumerians had a monosyllabic word for these prototypes of universal laws, the word *me* (pronounced "may"), whose precise meaning and etymology are still uncertain, though the recent study of the *me* by the young Sumerologist Gertrud Farber-Flügge (see footnote 7, Chapter 1, this volume) has brought some clarity. As she points out in this study, the *me* are described in the literary documents as "good," "pure," "holy," "great," "noble," "precise," "innumerable," "eternal," "awesome," "intricate," "untouchable"; they could be "presented," "given," "taken," "held," "lifted," "gathered," "worn"

30. The passage is from a hymn to Enki as an all-beneficent deity, a translation of which can be found in the third edition of *Ancient Near Eastern Texts*, pp. 573–580.
31. This passage is from "Enki and the World Order"; see p. 48 of this volume.

(like a garment), "fastened at the side," "directed," "perfected"; deities could sit upon them, put their feet upon them, ride upon them; they could even be loaded on a boat and carried off from one city to another.

The god who originally planned and devised these all-embracing *me* that produced and governed "law and order" in the universe was probably the heaven-god An. But by the time the relevant texts become available, some time in the second half of the third millennium B.C., An had become an obsolescent deity, and it was the air-god Enlil who was regarded by the theologians and mythographers as the deity who had originated the *me* and then turned them over to the water-god Enki for safekeeping in his watery shrine, the *Abzu*.

While it was An and Enlil who had planned the creation of everything essential to civilized life, it was Enki, the god of wisdom, as well as of seas and rivers, who organized the universe and made it operate as a going concern. The manner in which he did this is depicted in two major sources: the introduction to a composition that consists primarily of a disputation between the Bird and the Fish,[32] and a well-preserved, imaginative myth that describes Enki's skillful, systematic, and effective modus operandi.

The "Bird and Fish" passage is devoted primarily, but not entirely, to Enki's beneficent activities relating to the life-giving waters, thus:

After, in primeval days, a kindly fate had been decreed,
And of the cosmos, An and Enlil had established its rules,
Nudimmud, the noble prince, the lord of wide understanding,
Enki, the fate-decreeing king, being their third,
5 Collected all the waters, established their dwelling-places,
Let flow at his side the life-giving waters that begat the fecund seed,

32. See my translation of this composition in the *Compte Rendu* of the XI Rencontre Assyriologique (1962), based on an as yet unpublished edition of the text by Miguel Civil.

Suspended at his side the Tigris and Euphrates, brought into
   them the waters of all the lands,
Cleansed the small canals, made furrow-ditches alongside them.
Father Enki spread wide the stalls, provided them with shepherd
   and herdsman,
10 Founded cities and towns, multiplied the black-haired people,[33]
Provided the king for shepherdship over them, exalted him for
   princeship over them,
Made the king rise over the lands as a steadfast light.
The lord Enki organized the marshes, made grow there reeds
   young and old,
Brought fish and birds into the marshes, swamps, and lakes,
15 Filled the steppe with breathing creatures as their food and
   drink,
Charged them with supplying the abundance of the gods.
After Nudimmud, the noble prince, the lord of wide
   understanding,
Had fashioned the . . . ,
He filled the canebrake and marsh with fish and bird,
20 Assigned them to their stations,
Made them acquainted with the rules.[34]

33. Literally, "black-headed people," a designation for the Sumerians that is as
yet inexplicable.
34. The rather vague depiction of the Tigris and Euphrates in line 7 as the two
rivers surrounding Enki, who had collected and brought into them the waters of all
the lands, is quite different from that found in the myth "Enki and the World Order"
which portrays in concrete imagery Enki's filling of the Tigris with his semen as if it
were his loving bride, thus:

He [Enki] stands up proudly like a rampant bull,
He lifts his penis, ejaculates,
He fills the Tigris with sparkling waters,
The wild cow mooing for its young in the pastures.
The Tigris gave itself to him as to a rampant bull,
He lifted his penis, brought the bridal gift,
Brought joy to the Tigris, like a wild ox.

(For this passage, see for the present, *The Sumerians*, p. 179.)

As for the much more detailed myth of Enki's organizing activities, commonly designated "Enki and the World Order," I first pieced it together about twenty years ago from a number of tablets and fragments with the help of what is known in the trade as an "overseas join" of an eight-column tablet excavated almost a century ago by the University of Pennsylvania at Nippur, half of which came to the University Museum in Philadelphia while the other half found its way into the Hilprecht Sammlung of the Friedrich-Schiller University in Jena, East Germany. Its contents, recently edited more fully with the help of a number of newly identified duplicates by Carlos Benito, in a doctoral dissertation for the Oriental Department of the University of Pennsylvania, illustrate the Sumerian mythopoeic imagination at its most creative. It includes the god's glorification of his vast powers and prerogatives, and the creative power of his divine word and command; a description of his resplendent shrine, the *Abzu*, also known as the "Sea-House"; a sea journey to all the countries know to the Sumerians for the purpose of "decreeing their fate"; the assignment of appropriate deities to be in charge of the sea and the rivers; of the life-giving rain, of the plow, yoke, and furrow; of the cultivated field with its varied assortment of grains and vegetables; of the pickaxe and brickmold; of laying the foundations for houses and temples; of the verdant high steppe; of stalls and sheepfolds; of borders and boundaries; of weaving and cloth-making. Even so Enki had his troubles with the goddess Inanna, who complained that he had neglected her, that while he had provided a number of her sister deities with powers and insignia, he had failed to do so for her. Enki tries to pacify her by itemizing quite a number of powers and insignia that she did have. Unfortunately the very end of the myth is still quite fragmentary, and we must await its future recovery and restoration to learn whether or not the goddess was satisfied with Enki's response.

As is clear from the myths and mythological passages cited in this chapter, the creative acts of the Sumerian gods for the benefit of man and his welfare were manifold, reassuring, and awe-inspiring, though admittedly it was the gods' self-interest that motivated them in large part. They separated earth from heaven, so that life on earth could come into being, and illuminated earth with the light of the moon and its starry emanations; they vanquished the violent primeval chaos so dangerous to civilization and its progress; they filled the rivers with life-giving water, the steppes with four-legged creatures, the marshes with birds and fish, the fields with grain and vegetables; they even fashioned for man such utilitarian implements as the pickaxe and plow, the brickmold and spindle.

One very important creative contribution of the gods to man and his civilization, one that is rarely mentioned in the myths[35] but is a pervasive theme in the vast Sumerian hymnal repertoire, was the institution of kingship centering on the divinely chosen, charismatic ruler. As the next chapter will demonstrate, the poets and bards do not weary of singing the praises of the king as the shepherd, provider, and protector of his people, and as their representative before the gods. Beginning with a tentative historical sketch of the origin and development of kingship as a political and social institution, I continue with a brief analysis of the stylistic features of the royal hymns, and conclude with a portrait of the ideal ruler as envisaged and glorified by the ecstatic poets and bards.

35. See lines 9–12 of the passage cited on p. 47 of this work, according to which Enki provided the king for shepherdship over the Sumerian people after they had multiplied, and exalted him as a shining light over the land. For the mythological portrayal of the ruler as an incarnation of shepherd-king Dumuzi, the tragic spouse of Inanna, see p. 80 of this volume.

III

Glorification: A Royal Model of the Perfect Man

By the end of the third millennium B.C., the institution of kingship in Sumer had become the very hallmark of civilized society. As expected it had its *me*,[1] that is, the laws, limits, and controls relative to its authority and administration, its powers and its duties, as planned and assigned in the days of the creation of the universe. In a manner of speaking, the Sumerian theologians and mythographers summed it all up with the statement "Kingship descended from heaven."[2] They seem to have assumed that is came "full blown, full grown," to Sumer. It is hardly likely that any of the Sumerian men of letters, even the most erudite and imaginative among them, conceived of kingship as an institution that had begun from scratch, as it were, and had evolved and developed over the centuries to the stage it had reached in the late third millennium B.C. The rise and growth of the institution of kingship is a social, economic, cultural, and historical phenomenon that the modern scholar must try to explain and verify from the excavated inscriptions and artifacts, and this is a rather thankless task since none of these is very informative and revealing. There is, therefore, much that is uncertain and subjective in this rather elusive inquiry,

---

1. This is the myth "Inanna and Enki: The Transfer of the *me* from Eridu to Erech" (see pp. 4, 5 of this volume); the *me* for kingship and its symbols and insignia are mentioned near the very beginning of the document.

2. See *The Sumerians*, p. 328.

and there is considerable room for differences and divergences in the relevant surmises, hypotheses, and conclusions.[3]

Right from the start, the historian is confronted by a problem crucial to the inquiry, one that is still a matter of controversy among the specialists in Ancient Near Eastern research. This is the well-known and often discussed question concerning the identity of the first settlers of the land, generally assumed to have arrived there some time in the fifth millennium B.C. Were these Sumerians, that is, a people who spoke the Sumerian language, or were they some other linguistic group or groups who were later superseded by the Sumerians, just as much later, the Sumerians were superseded by the Semitic people commonly known as Babylonians? This is not the place to discuss this complex problem in detail; a comprehensive and informative overview of the pros and cons has been published by Tom Jones of the University of Minnesota in his *The Sumerian Problem* (1969). Let me state only that I am one of those scholars who are of the opinion that the Sumerians were *not* the first in the land that in the third millennium B.C. came to be known as Sumer, later as Sumer and Akkad, and still later as Babylonia. It is my conviction that the earliest settlers in the land were a people who spoke neither Sumerian nor a Semitic tongue, but rather an as yet unidentified language that left its traces in the river name *idiglat* for the Tigris and *buranun* for the Euphrates; in such place names as Eridu, Ur, Larsam, Isin, Adab, Kullab, Lagash, and Nippur, none of which has a satisfactory Sumerian etymology; and even more important, in such cultural words as *engar* (farmer), *apin* (plow), *apsin* (furrow), *nimbar* (palm), *tibir* (metal worker), *simug* (smith), and perhaps even *damkar* (merchant), a word that has generally been taken to be a Semitic hallmark.[4]

3. See, for example, Henri Frankfort, *The Birth of Civilization* (1956), pp. 68–70, and Thorkild Jacobsen, *Toward the Image of Tammuz* (1970), pp. 132–156.

4. The recognition that these crucial cultural words were neither Sumerian nor Semitic is due principally to the penetrating insight of the late Benno Landsberger; see *Undena Publications, Sources and Monographs*, vol. 1, fascicle 2 (1974), pp. 8–12.

This non-Sumerian, non-Semitic people, I venture to suggest, came to settle in southern Mesopotamia as pioneering colonists from the north or east in search of a new home in the alluvial plain of the Tigris and the Euphrates. To be sure, southern Mesopotamia in the early fifth millennium could hardly be described as a land flowing with milk and honey—it was no doubt a bleak and dismal region of desert, swamp, and marsh. But these early colonists had little to lose and much to gain by leaving their agricultural villages and emigrating in search of new homes. I would surmise that, not unlike the first Europeans to settle in America, these Near Eastern pioneers were individuals and families who abandoned their homes because they belonged to the economically oppressed and depressed, to the disgruntled and dissatisfied; some of them may even have been religious dissidents who felt themselves out of place in their home villages and towns.[5]

But granted that these early pioneers had good reason to seek new homes, why were they attracted to the hot, dry, parched, windswept, flood-prone land between the Tigris and Euphrates, and how was it that they took root and stayed there, and in the course of the centuries turned it into a veritable "Garden of Eden"? The answer is to be found in a physical feature related to the two rivers that was an invaluable boon to the immigrating agriculturists with their pots and pans, their stone tools and implements, their precious seed and flour that they must have brought with them from their abandoned homes. Dominating the low-lying alluvial plain were relatively high levees strung all along the meandering Euphrates, built up over the millennia by the river as it repeatedly overtopped its banks. These levees with their gentle backslopes of course-textured silt and sediment lent themselves readily to draining, planting, and cultivation, and so were ideal for the kind of simple agriculture known and practiced by these primitive farmers. Most important, they lay close to the river, the sole source of water

5. I first proposed this hypothesis and analogy in *The Cradle of Civilization* (1967), p. 16.

for irrigation and household use during the hot, dry summer months. Then, too, not far from the levees were numerous reed-covered swamps and marshes formed by the river's overflow into the irregular depressions characteristic of this plain. During much of the year, these supported a rich fauna that could be hunted for meat and skin, while in the spring they provided abundant forage for large herds of sheep and goats. It is not surprising, therefore, that it was alongside these promising natural levees along the Euphrates that the first settlers decided to establish themselves, and that they gradually became prosperous and flourishing agriculturists.[6]

These original settlers of Sumer, now generally designated as Ubaidians, or Proto-Euphrateans,[7] became a significant cultural and civilizing force in Lower Mesopotamia, and traces of their influence have been found over the entire Ancient Near East.[8] But, to return to the institution of kingship, it is very unlikely that they were ruled by a king or that they knew anything of royal dynasties, legitimate or otherwise; there was hardly the economic, social, political need for the institution of kingship during the fifth and much or all of the fourth millennium B.C. To be sure, there is no way of knowing this with absolute certainty, but a reasonable hypothesis that could explain and illuminate the rise of kingship would, to my mind, run approximately as follows:

When the first immigrants into Southern Mesopotamia settled on the gentle slopes of the Euphrates levees, they struck "pay-dirt" immediately; the seed they planted in the easily plowed, fertile soil

6. The importance of this topographical feature for Sumer's earliest agriculturists was first suggested by Robert Adams in his more recent publications; see Assyriological Bibliography in *Orientalia* for relevant items.

7. The name *Ubaidian* derives from the small mound near Ur, known as Tell Ubaid, where the archeological traces of these early settlers were first unearthed. The name Proto-Euphratean was first proposed by Benno Landsberger (see footnote 4, this chapter).

8. See James Mellaart, *The Neolithic of the Near East* (1975), pp. 176–179, and Joan Oates, *Iraq*, vol. 22 (1970), pp. 32–50, and especially her report in the XXIV Rencontre Assyriologique (Paris, 1977) entitled "The Seafaring Merchants of Ur (?)."

yielded a rich and manifold return. To be sure, there were dark days when the river overflowed its banks so violently that it flooded and drowned everything within its reach. But usually the inundation was moderate and gentle, and could be readily channeled into the small canals and primitive reservoirs that even the very first "Ubaidians" had learned to construct. With food plentiful and reasonably assured, families grew in size—the more children, the larger the field that could be cultivated—and the original hamlet consisting of several flimsy reed huts gradually developed into a village of mud-brick houses with several rooms each. What had begun as a family enterprise became a small local community in which attachment to place gradually became the prime incentive of all major activity. It was this shift of loyalty, slow but sure, from kin to neighbor, from family to group, that was of fundamental significance for the rise of the city and its subsequent growth and development.

There was at least one other presence in the early village that made the role of the community as a whole paramount—the temple and its services. The first immigrants into southern Mesopotamia either brought with them or developed not long after their arrival a trusting faith in one special deity as the protector and guardian of their settlement—so much so, that with the building of their first houses, they also erected a home for the divinity who was uniquely theirs. In Eridu, for example, the excavators unearthed a mud-brick temple built by the "Ubaidians" on virgin soil.[9] It was a small shrine, less than four meters square, and its religious furnishings consisted of nothing more than an altar and an offering table. But as the village grew it was gradually enlarged into an elaborate structure erected on a lofty platform. This temple served the community as a whole, not an individual family or clan, and this generated and intensified local patriotism and pride.

9. See Seton Lloyd and Fuad Safar, Sumer IV, pp. 115–127.

The temple, moreover, was not just dry, lifeless brick and mortar: it was a venerated, sacred place of worship that had to be tended and cared for day in, day out, year in, year out; hymns and prayers had to be composed, formalized, and recited; rites and rituals, be they ever so primitive, had to be performed; holy days had to be celebrated. And so a specialized priesthood came into being, beginning no doubt with the selection and appointment of one or two individuals noted for their spiritual powers and charismatic gifts, and proliferating in number and function over the centuries. It was the temple and its priestly coterie that naturally became the intellectual center of the community, and not surprisingly it was in the temple that writing was first invented and developed. To be sure, it was the economic rather than the spiritual needs of the temple that promoted some of its personnel to devise a system of writing essential for the accountancy and control over the vast wealth that accrued to it over the years through gifts and bequests of the more wealthy citizens of the community. Once introduced, however, it led to the development of a formal system of education, and literacy became a prime characteristic of the urban way of life. It was in the temples and schools of the cities of Sumer that the educated, literate man was born, the prototype of the modern intellectual, writer, teacher, and scholar.[10]

Nor did priests and temple managers long remain the only specialized functionaries of the early communities of southern Mesopotamia. For as the villages prospered and expanded, so did the size and number of their farms and fields, as well as of their canals and reservoirs. These latter were absolutely essential to their agricultural economy; without them the land would revert to barren desert in this virtually rainless region. But irrigation, especially in its more advanced stages, can be effectively carried out only as a community enterprise, not as an individual undertaking. Canals

10. See chapter 6 of *The Sumerians*.

and reservoirs of considerable size had to be excavated, cleaned at regular intervals, and kept in a constant state of repair; water rights had to be distributed fairly and equitably; boundary lines had to be carefully marked and authenticated; arguments and disputes—and these were no doubt endemic in these enterprising, property-oriented communities—had to be adjudicated and settled. All of which led to the gradual rise of a secular administration center beginning with limited appointed personnel but developing over the centuries into a formidable bureaucracy with all the advantages and evils that this entails.

As long as the communities remained in their village stage, and the land and irrigation conflicts were confined to individuals and families, the secular administration played a minor role in community life and was no threat to the individual's freedom; objectionable and untrustworthy officials could be readily removed from office by the citizen assemblies that met from time to time as the need arose.[11] But as more prosperous, successful, and enterprising villages grew into towns, and the towns to cities, each eager to own and control as much as possible of the rich, irrigated land in and about its borders, strife and contention become ever more violent, virulent, and fraught with disastrous consequences for the loser. Whole communities of considerable size and number were now involved, and the stakes were high. What had started largely as limited economic rivalry turned into a bitter political struggle for power, prestige, and territory.[12] A taste for dominance and domination had gradually developed among the more possessive, aggressive, and predatory communities, and these turned to warfare and weaponry to achieve their ambitious goals. Unable to cope with such perilous military threats, the "democratic" assemblies, the

11. For these early assemblies and the manner in which they may have functioned, see especially Thorkild Jacobsen, *Towards the Image of Tammuz*, pp. 157–172.

12. For a graphic example of this kind of bitter struggle in the destructive civil war between the cities of Lagash and Umma that lasted for several generations, see *The Sumerians*, pp. 53–58.

decision-making bodies of the early villages and towns, turned over some of their powers and prerogatives to one or another of their more capable and resourceful citizens, their courageous and responsible "big men," to lead them to victory over their enemy. And so the king was born and the institution of kingship came into being. At first the king's appointment was no doubt temporary and his powers were limited; with the passing of the military crisis, he returned to civic life as an ordinary member of the community, honored and esteemed for his services. But as conflict bred conflict, and war bred war, kingship lost its transitory character and became hereditary, dynastic, and in some cases despotic.

Who the first king was in Sumer is unknown at present, and it is very unlikely that it can ever be known with reasonable certainty. There are some indications that he may have been a Semite, for there is good reason to surmise that Semitic nomads from Syria and Arabia had infiltrated the Ubaidian settlements as peaceful immigrants and as warlike conquerors long before the arrival of the Sumerians.[13] According to our only available source for this point in time, the so-called Sumerian "Kinglist,"[14] the first dynasty after the legendary Flood was that of the city of Kish, and its earliest rulers bear Semitic names.

The actual word for king, the Sumerian compound *lu-gal*, "Big Man," is first found in the semipictographic inscriptions excavated by the Germans at Erech that date from approximately 3000 B.C.[15] But nothing is known of the king's role from contemporary sources until some centuries later. Even then, it is not the royal inscriptions that provide any significant information, but the onomasticon current in archaic Ur, Shuruppak, and the ancient town covered by

13. See ibid., p. 42.
14. This document was edited with great care in 1941 by Thorkild Jacobsen in his monograph entitled *The Sumerian King List*. In 1952 the eminent Leiden cuneiformist F. R. Kraus made a number of significant corrections to this monograph (see *Zeitschrift fur Assyriologie*, vol. 50, pp. 29–60), and these are included in my translation of the document in *The Sumerians*, pp. 328–331.
15. See Adam Falkenstein, *Archäische Texte aus Uruk* (1936).

the *tell* known as Abu Salabih. As the Munich cuneiformist Dietz Edzard has pointed out in his paper on kingship in predynastic times published in the *Proceedings* of the XIX Rencontre Assyriologique Internationale (1974), the names given to Sumerian children of those early days are quite revealing for the king and his royal functions. Such names as *lugal-ur-sag*, "the king is a warrior," *lugal-engar*, "the king is a farmer," *lugal-a-mah*, "the king (possesses) noble might," *lugal-si-sa*, "the king (exercises) justice," *lugal-he-gal*, "the king (brings about) prosperity," *lugal-za-da*, "*Oh king (who is there) beside you*," *lugal-u-su-she*, "may the king (live) unto distant days," *lugal-u-ma*, "the king (stands) triumphant," indicate clearly that the ruler was regarded with admiration and reverence, with faith and trust in his deeds and achievements. It is not unreasonable to conclude, therefore, that in the early third millennium B.C. the institution of kingship was a fully established, going concern.

From this time on, right down to the days of Hammurabi, that is, for more than a millennium, we have hundreds of building and votive royal inscriptions on tablets of clay and stone, on bricks and door-sockets, on bowls and vases, on clay nails and cones, on mortars and maceheads, on plaques and steles, on statues and statuettes of stone and metal, on administrative tablets inscribed with date formulas recording important religious and political events.[16] All of these, together with the legendary epic tales and historiographic compositions,[17] are quite informative and illuminating about the deeds and achievements of the Sumerian kings, their victories and defeats, their successes and failures, their rosy expectations and bitter disappointments. We are even fortunate enough to have some of the royal correspondence, the letters that went back and forth between the rulers and their high officials,

16. Most of these have been collected and translated in the valuable up-to-date handbook *Inscriptions Royales Sumériennes et Akkadiennes* (1971) by Edmond Sollberger and Jean-Robert Kupper.
17. See Chapter 5 of *The Sumerians* for details.

and these reveal the temptations, rivalries, and intrigues that pervaded the royal court and at times embittered the king's life and spirit.[18] From all these historical and semihistorical documents, it is abundantly clear that there were all kinds of Sumerian kings: good and bad, wise and foolish, ambitious and complacent, energetic and lethargic, resolute and vacillating, courageous and cowardly, benign and cruel, generous and niggardly. In physical appearance too[19]—unfortunately we have no real portraits of the kings, only formalized and conventionalized representations—the rulers no doubt varied significantly in size and shape, in grace and elegance, in charm and attractiveness.

But different as they may have been, they had one psychological trait in common; they all seem to have had a compulsive need and obsessive drive for glorification and celebration, for fame and name, for appreciation and acclaim, for repute and renown. In very early days, long before writing had become an effective tool of communication, the court minstrels and bards sang their ruler's praises accompanied by such musical instruments as the harp and the lyre.[20] With the development of the cuneiform script, some of these hymns and songs began to be written down, though as of today very little of these earlier compositions has been recovered. Beginning with Ur-Nammu, however, the king who founded the Third Dynasty of Ur, and continuing right down to Hammurabi and his son Samsu-iluna, the royal hymns become ever more numerous and stereotyped. Throughout this long period of some

18. See Fadhil Ali, *Sumerian Letters* (1965), and *The Sumerians*, pp. 331–335.

19. The statues, statuettes, and stelas of quite a number of the Sumerian rulers can be found in Andre Parrot's *Sumer* (1960) (for example, pp. 130, 135, 177, 206, 218, 228, 303). With the possible exception of Gudea, none of these is a true portrait of the king which it is intended to represent.

20. For depictions of these early minstrels, see for example the "symposium" plaque illustrated in *Sumer*, pp. 132, 197. An extraordinary statuette that may be an actual portrait of a blind minstrel is that of Ur-Nanshe (*Sumer*, pp. 26 and 27); that some minstrels in Sumer may have been blind is evident from the myth concerned with the creation of man, according to which the god Enki gave the "art of song" to the blind man fashioned by the goddess Ninmah (see p. 20 of this volume).

five centuries, the court poets who were educated and trained in the *edubba*, the Sumerian academy that must have been supported in part by the king himself, composed a varied assortment of royal hymns that glorify the ruler in hyperbolic diction and extravagant imagery; they tell us very little about the true character and authentic historical achievements of the king with which the hymn is concerned, but are quite revealing for the ideal type of ruler that the people must have envisaged and longed for. I shall conclude this section with an analysis of some of the more significant relevant statements that help to depict in one way or another the attributes and qualities, the powers and duties, the deeds and achievements of the ruler that should have been, but never was.[21]

To start with the ideal king's embryonic beginnings, it is of interest to note that the poets who composed the royal hymns conceived of his birth on two levels, the human and the divine, and it was the latter rather than the former that was close to their hearts—hardly ever do they mention the name of the real parents of the king. On the divine level, on the other hand, the hymnal poets rarely fail to mention the ruler's parentage, although the relevant statements are usually rather brief and at times contradictory, or seemingly so. In the case of the kings of the Third Dynasty of Ur, the divine parents are Lugalbanda[22] and his wife the goddess Ninsun. In the case of the later kings, the parents were usually said to be the great god Enlil and his wife Ninlil, although Hammurabi boasts of Marduk as his father.

One of the more poetic stylistic features of the royal hymns consists of utilizing an imaginative symbolism taken primarily from the animal kingdom and more rarely from the world of vegetation. Thus in connection with the royal birth, a king may be described as a "true offspring engendered by a bull, speckled of head and body";

21. For bibliographical references, see the *Compte rendu* of the XIX Rencontre Assyriologique (1976), pp. 163–176.
22. Lugalbanda is one of the heroes of Sumer who was deified in later days.

"a calf of an all-white cow, thick of neck, raised in a stall"; "a king born of a wild cow, nourished(?) on cream and milk"; "a calf born in a stall of plenty"; "a young bull born in a year of plenty, fed on rich milk in halcyon days"; "a fierce-eyed lion born of a dragon"; "a fierce panther(?) fed on rich milk"; "a thick-horned bull born to a big lion"; "a mighty warrior born to a lion."

The king came into the world blessed from the womb, if we take literally such exulting phrases as "from the womb of my mother Ninsun a sweet blessing went forth for me"; "I am a warrior from the womb, I am a mighty man from birth"; "I am a noble son blessed from the womb"; "I am a king adored, a fecund seed from the womb"; "a prince fit(?) for kingship from the fecund womb." But it must have been during, or following, his coronation, or when he was about to conduct a campaign against the enemy that the poets envisaged him as receiving various divine blessings, most frequently from Enlil of Nippur. Usually this came about through the intervention of another deity. A vivid, concrete example of this procedure as imagined by the poets is provided by a hymn to Shulgi which states that the king "on the day he had been raised to kingship" came before Nanna, the tutelary deity of Ur, with a promise to joyfully restore the *me*.[23] Whereupon the god journeyed to Nippur, entered the Ekur where he was greeted by the assembly of the gods, and addressed Enlil as follows:

Father Enlil, lord whose command cannot be turned back,
Father of the gods who established the *me*,
You have lifted your face upon my city, you have decreed the
    fate of Ur,
Bless the just king whom I have called to my holy heart,
5 The king, the shepherd Shulgi, the faithful shepherd full of
    grace,
Let him subjugate the promised land for me.

23. For the rulers mentioned throughout these pages, see the index to the *Sumerians* and to Dietz Edzard's *Die zweite zwischenzeit Babylonians* (1957).

Enlil, the poet continues, responded favorably to Nanna's plea, and the god returned to Ur with Enlil's blessing and said to Shulgi:

Enlil has perfected for you the might of the land,
Son of Ninsun, king, shepherd Shulgi, may your scepter reach afar.

According to the author of this hymn, Nanna went alone to the Ekur to obtain the blessing for Shulgi; the king himself stayed in Ur. But there are hymns that depict the intervening deity taking the king along to receive the blessing directly from Enlil's mouth. Thus, according to a hymn concerned with Ishme-Dagan, the king is brought to the Ekur by the goddess Bau who asks for his blessing, which Enlil proceeds to pronounce in words that summarize succinctly everything essential for an ideal reign: a throne that gathers all the *me*; an enduring crown; a scepter that exercises firm control over the people; overflow of the rivers; fertility of the womb and soil; a name famous and glorious; tribute from the lands near and far; the sending of perennial gifts to the Ekur of Nippur.

Another hymn, one that is even more instructive for the concrete, realistic manner in which the poets envisioned the king's divine benediction, involves the goddess Inanna and her royal husband Ur-Ninurta. This composition begins by stating that Inanna, having made up her mind to see to it that the *me* of kingship be restored and that the "black-haired people" be properly guided and governed, has chosen Ur-Ninurta as the shepherd over all the people. Powerful goddess though she was, she nevertheless deems it necessary to first obtain for him the blessings of An and Enlil, both of whom reside in the Ekur of Nippur. She therefore takes the king by the hand, brings him to the Ekur, and implores the two deities for their benediction. An responds first with a series of blessings addressed directly to the king, and Enlil follows with his benediction. After the assembly of the gods in Nippur had said "Amen" to these blessings, Inanna turned over to Ur-Ninurta all the "lofty" *me*, and the two of them left the Ekur together for their own domicile where the goddess further eulogizes the king as the blessed of Enlil.

The king, however, did not always have the need of a deity to intervene in his behalf; he could journey all alone to receive blessings from various gods. Shulgi, for example, according to one hymn, traveled by boat first to Erech, where following the performance of the "Sacred Marriage" rite, Inanna blesses and exalts him as the one truly fit for royalty in all its aspects. From Erech he continues his journey to two other cities and is blessed and exalted by their tutelary deities. Finally he arrives in his own city Ur, where he presents offerings to Nanna and is further extolled and blessed.

Between the king's birth and his coronation were the days of his childhood and adolescence, and the modern historian is eager for information about the education and upbringing of the king-to-be. But as of today there is only one hymn that intimates anything at all about the young prince's education, and that only in a very brief passage. However, if taken at its face value, or even if true in part only, its content is most enlightening and culturally invaluable. Here is what, according to this hymn, the king Shulgi has to say about his education:

During my youth there was the *edubba* [school] where
On the tablets of Sumer and Akkad I learned the scribal art,
No youth could write as well as I on clay,
I was instructed in the learned places of the scribal art,
5 I am accomplished in subtraction, addition, counting, and
　　accounting,
The gracious Nanibgal, the goddess Nidaba, ...
Has given me generously of wisdom and understanding,
I am a dextrous scribe whom nothing impedes.

In short, this king, if we trust the hymn, was himself one of the most literate and erudite personages of his realm.

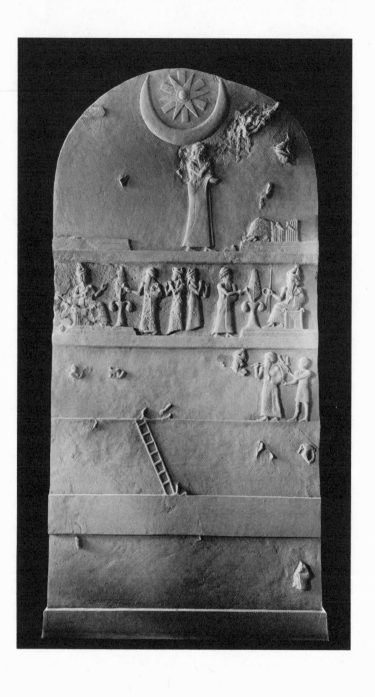

Glorification

A few rather vague "human-interest" particulars about the life of a very young prince and the motherly love that enveloped it may be gathered from a composition that is not a hymn but a lullaby purported to be sung by the wife of Shulgi to her ill and restless son. In this poem we read of the mother rocking her son to sleep, as it were, with wistful, reassuring chants and promises of sweet little cheeses and well-watered lettuce, as well as with such blessings as a loving wife and beloved children attended by a joyous nursemaid, abundance of food, good angels, and a happy reign once he comes to the throne.

But whatever his education and upbringing, the king of Sumer and Akkad was the perfect, ideal man: physically powerful and distinguished-looking, intellectually without peer, spiritually a paragon of piety and probity. Thus, to take his physical appearance, Ur-Nammu is a "comely lord" invested with grace and a halo of splendor. Shulgi has a comely mouth and a countenance most fair; his "lapis lazuli" beard overlaying his holy chest is a wonder to behold; his majestic appearance qualifies him eminently for dais and throne, and for the precious regalia that cover him from the crown on his head to the sandals on his feet. Lipit-Ishtar has a "lapis lazuli" beard, a fair countenance, a comely mouth that makes bright the heart, a figure full of grace, lips that are the ornament of speech, fingers fair—he is a virile man sweet to gaze at.

Opposite page. Limestone stele (excavated by Leonard Woolley at Ur and now in the University Museum at the University of Pennsylvania) of Ur-Nammu, founder of the Third Dynasty of Ur (about 2100 B.C.) and history's first recorded law-giver. The stele, which is about 10 feet high, depicts scenes from the king's preparation for building the ziggurat (stepped tower) of Ur, dedicated to the moon-god Nanna and his wife Ningal. The second panel shows the king watering a plant, symbolizing perhaps the tree of life, before the two seated deities, while the third panel shows him carrying building implements over his shoulder, supported by a servant. With the permission of the Photographic Department of the University Museum, University of Pennsylvania.

Ur-Ninurta is a comely, virile man with fair limbs, he is full of grace, an ornament of lordship. Rim-Sin has a graceful forehead, princely limbs, a tall figure. Even more impressive than his majestic appearance were the king's physical powers, his courage and bravery. Shulgi, for example, is a warrior from the womb, a mighty man from the day he was born; his god Nanna gave him "warriorship" and might in his temple; Enlil gave him a "lofty arm"; he is a mighty king always in the vanguard; he is a mighty warrior born to a lion; he is a king of preeminent strength, who exercises firmly his "warriorship" and who glorifies in song his strength and his might.

The importance attributed to the king's physique and courage is evidenced by the rich imagery and symbolism evolved by the hymnal poets: Shulgi is a lion with wide-open mouth; a great wild bull with powerful limbs; a dragon with the face of a lion; he is as strong as an oak(?) planted by the water-course; a fertile *mes*-tree[24] bedecked with fruit, sweet to gaze at. Ishme-Dagan is a tall *mes*-tree, thick of root and wide of branch, a lofty mountain(?) that cannot be touched; he flashes brightly over the land like electrum(?); he is a cedar-shoot planted in a cedar forest; he is luxuriant like the boxwood-tree. Lipit-Ishtar holds high his head like a cedar-shoot; he is a lion on the prowl that has no rival, an open-mouthed dragon that is the terror of the troops, a wild bull whom none dares attack.

The powerful physique and heroic bravery of the king were naturally of vital importance for victory in the recurrent destructive wars that plagued Sumer. Many of the prayers interspersed in the royal hymns are for victory in war, and it is in connection with war that the poets evolved some of their more extravagent imagery: Shulgi is a torrent thundering against the rebellious land; his weapon grinds its teeth like a sharp-toothed beast; his fierce weapon pours out venom like a snake all set for the bite; his arrows fly into

24. The *mes*-tree is an as yet unidentified fruit tree.

the battle like flying bats; his bow pierces like a dragon; he is a warrior in battle who knows no rival, a dragon whose tongue darts out against the enemy; he speeds to subdue the enemy like a lion. Ishme-Dagon is "a warrior of warriors," the wrath of weapons. Lipit-Ishtar is an attacking floodwave in battle; he flashes like lightning. Ur-Ninurta rages like a storm against the enemy; his halo of splendor covers the rebellious land like a heavy cloud.

Related to the king's prowess in war was his skill in the chase. Shulgi boasts that he hunts lions in the steppe man to man, as it were, without the aid of a net or an enclosure; he simply waits until the beast opens its mouth and hurls the spear-point into it. He claims to be so fast on his feet that he can catch a running gazelle.

The king was endowed with great wisdom and profound understanding as well as with physical prowess and heroic courage. Virtually all the kings in the hymnal repertoire were said to be endowed with wisdom by Enki, the god of wisdom, and with learning by Nidaba, the goddess of writing. The king was also psychologically penetrating and astute: he could give wise and eloquent counsel in the assembly; he could seek and find the wise word; he could discern "the words that were in the heart" to determine the true from the false; he cooled "the hot heart" and "put an end to the burning word." He had a great love for music and song, both of which he knew expertly and practiced diligently. At least this was true of Shulgi—a goodly part of at least two Shulgi hymns depict his devotion to music, both instrumental and vocal.

Spiritually, the achievements of the king concerned two major areas: religion and social behavior. In the sphere of religion, it was the ruler's devotion to the cult that in the main interested the hymnal poets. The king knew how to serve the gods and saw to it that the temple rites and rituals were properly consummated, that libations were offered daily as well as during the various monthly holidays and New Year's day, when the king's sacred marriage to Inanna was celebrated. Shulgi also claims that he could himself interpret oracles, carry out perfectly the lustration rites, fill the high priestly offices in accordance with the omens, and read the precious words of the gods before going to war by examining the entrails of a white sheep. The hymns on the whole leave the impression that the king cared for the cult in each of the more important religious centers of Sumer. But it was the Ekur of Nippur that was uppermost in his mind; virtually every king in the repertoire brought gifts, offerings, and sacrifices to Enlil in his temple.

Social justice, equity, and law were, according to the hymns, a prime concern of the ruler, since Sumerian society was polarized into rich and poor, strong and weak, powerful and impotent. Usually the relevant statements are brief and general, but some are more specific and detailed. Ishme-Dagan, for example, asserts that he was a judge who did not tolerate iniquity, that he did not permit the powerful to oppress the weak nor the noble to mistreat the ordinary citizen, that under his sign the poor dared talk back to the rich, that there was no bribed verdict or twisted words, that the cry of the wronged, the widow, and the orphan were not in vain.

The society of Sumer also suffered from the "generation gap" that plagues modern society, and several of the kings claim to have done something about it. Shulgi, for example, saw to it that mother spoke kindly to the son, and that the son answered truthfully to his father. Ishme-Dagan alleges that during his reign "brother speaks the truth to brother," "the father is respected," "the older sister is not contradicted," "the mother is feared."

The Oriental monarchs, including those of Sumer, are often cited by the modern historian as striking examples of despotic tyrants: cruel, oppressive, ruthless. This is certainly not how the Sumerian poets viewed their rulers; as they saw it, all the king's actions—conducting wars, constructing temples, maintaining the cult, digging and restoring canals, building and repairing highways, promulgating law codes—all had one supreme goal: to make the people happy, prosperous, and secure. This theme is an ever-recurring motif in the hymns: the king is the farmer who fills the granaries, the shepherd who enriches the stalls and the sheepfolds; he is the high protecting wall of the land; the people look up to him as their father and live securely in his sweet shade. In brief, to quote the oft-repeated summary phrase of the poet, he "makes sweet the flesh of the people." To be sure this was not his sole motive; there was at least one other significant source of inspiration for the ruler's brave, wise, pious, and benevolent deeds: an obsessive, ambitious drive for fame and name. Throughout their hymns, the poets, who obviously had a vested interest in the glorification of the king and the celebration of his achievements, do not tire of reiterating that as a result of his unrivaled accomplishments, his "sweet" and "noble" name will be honored and exalted in all the lands unto distant days, especially by the scribes of the *edubba*, that is, by poets and men of letters like themselves.

So much for the ideal king as glorified and exalted by the poets and bards. Though the authors of the royal hymns did not intend it, indirectly and inferentially they provided us with an impressive, revealing portrait of the ideal man in general, the type of individual whom the ordinary Sumerian might have liked to see his son imitate and emulate: distinguished looking, charmismatic, intelligent, astute, learned, eloquent, daring, courageous, just, kind, pious. Unfortunately, as in the case of the ideal king, the ideal man existed only in the visionary imagination and utopian dreamworld. For, as I tried to demonstrate in a paper read before the XVIII Rencontre Assyriologique held in Munich in 1970, Sumerian society, not unlike our own tormented society, had its deplorable failings and distressing shortcomings. Nevertheless it is not unreasonable to surmise that there were at least some Sumerians who, consciously or unconsciously, strove to become the ideal man of the poetic imagination and to cultivate at least some of the virtues, qualities, and achievements exemplified in the noble and exalted ethic attested by the royal hymns.

The cultic role in which the king no doubt delighted most was the part he played as the incarnatic of the shepherd-king Dumuzi in the Sacred Marriage rite, which culminated in his ecstatic sexual union with Inanna, the passionate and desirable goddess of love.[25] But this fertility rite featured only one aspect of this fascinating deity, whose complex and multifaceted character will be sketched and analyzed in the next chapter.

25. For the origin and evolution of this fertility cult, see *The Sacred Marriage Rite*, pp. 49–66.

IV

Adoration: A Divine Model of the Liberated Woman

Female deities were worshipped and adored all through Sumerian history, and though several of them, as noted in an earlier chapter, were victimized and reduced in hierarchical rank, the goddesses of Sumer played a crucial, pivotal role in Sumerian religion to the very end—God in Sumer never became all male. To mention some of the more prestigious among them, the deity in charge of writing, learning, and accounting was a goddess by the name of Nidaba; the deity in charge of medicine and healing was a goddess worshipped under various names such as Bau and Ninisinna; the deity that was Sumer's social conscience, who judged mankind on New Year's day, and who saw to it that the weak, the poor, the oppressed, the widow, and the orphan were looked after and cared for, was a goddess by the name of Nanshe.[1] But the goddess who outweighed, overshadowed, and outlasted them all was a deity known to the Sumerians by the name of Inanna, "Queen of Heaven," and to the Semites who lived in Sumer by the name of Ishtar.[2]

Inanna played a greater role in myth, epic, and hymn than any other deity, male or female. And no wonder, for she was worshipped under three aspects that at least on the surface seem

1. See *The Legacy of Sumer* (Denise Schmandt-Besserat, ed., 1976), pp. 13–17, for fuller details.
2. The name Esther is a dialectal pronunciation of Ishtar.

unrelated, and even antithetical: as the Venus-goddess in charge of the bright Morning Star and Evening Star; as the goddess of war and weaponry, who wrought havoc upon all who displeased her, and especially on the enemies of Sumer; as the goddess of love and desire who ensured the fertility of the soil and the fecundity of the womb.

Let me begin with the epic tales, where we find Inanna mentioned in most, and a major protagonist in some. To date there are available nine Sumerian epic tales, four centering on the heroes Enmerkar and Lugalbanda, and five on Mesopotamia's hero par excellence, Gilgamesh.[3] One Enmerkar tale is particularly noteworthy since it includes what may be described as a prototype of the "Helen of Troy" motif: the love of Inanna was the prize of the victor Enmerkar, who had carried off the goddess from Aratta, a still unidentified city in ancient Iran, to his own city, Erech, and thus may have sparked a state of war between these two cities.

In another Enmerkar tale, the goddess is represented as the main support of the hero in his challenging demand that the people of Aratta send some of the precious metals and stones in which their highland city abounded to build several shrines for him in Erech and Eridu. According to a third Enmerkar tale, the goddess, for some unknown reason, had abandoned the hero and his city in a moment of crisis, and came to his aid only after Enmerkar had sent her a reproachful message carried by his loyal, brave liegeman, Lugalbanda.

3. For the sketch of the contents of the Sumerian epic tales, and for translation of some of them, see *The Sumerians*, pp. 184–205.

Opposite page: *Wall painting from one of the courts of Mari, the ancient Mesopotamian city excavated by André Parrot. The upper scene of the central panel depicts the goddess Inanna-Ishtar presenting the "line and rod," the emblems of royalty, to the king of Mari. (The other panels in the painting depict scenes whose religious and symbolic meaning is uncertain.) With the permission of the Photographic Department of the Louvre, Paris.*

This Lugalbanda is the major protagonist in the fourth epic tale, in which he is depicted as a solitary, wandering hero, and though the goddess plays no role whatever in the plot of this tale, she is not left out altogether. When Lugalbanda, sick to death, abandoned by his brothers and friends in *hurrum-kur-ra* (probably a mountain cave), raised his tear-filled eyes to the heavens and prayed to the gods for his recovery, one of his entreaties was addressed to Inanna, whom the poet depicts in these words:

> To the harlot who in the tavern makes slumber sweet,
> To her who provides food for the poor,
> To Inanna, the daughter of Sin,
> Who like a bull lifts her head in the land . . . . ,
> 5 Whose countenance lights up the mountain cave,
> To Inanna, to whom he lifted his eyes,
> He pleaded tearfully as if to the father who begot him,
> In the mountain cave he raised his comely hands.

In the Gilgamesh cycle, Inanna plays a significant role in only two tales and these reveal, rather unexpectedly, an anomalous and ambivalent relationship between the goddess and the hero. In "Gilgamesh, Enkidu, and the Nether World," the poem whose plot I sketched in the second chapter, we see the goddess, whose *huluppu*-tree had been infested with pernicious monsters, entreating the hero to come to her aid and rewarding him for his brave deliverance of the tree at the risk of his life. How surprising, therefore, to find in another Gilgamesh epic tale, "Gilgamesh and the Bull of Heaven," that, angered by the hero's rejection of her proffered love and riches, she is determined to put him to death and wreak havoc on his city Erech, although she was its tutelary deity and though it was the home of her far-famed sanctuary. To achieve her vindictive purpose, she appealed to the heaven-god An to give her the *gud-an-na*, the "Bull of Heaven," that she might send him down on earth to ravage Erech. An at first refused, but terrified by the goddess's dire threats, he accedes to her request and turns over the "Bull of Heaven" to her. The end of this Sumerian tale is still missing, but to judge from the version in the Akkadian Epic of Gilgamesh which, it may be reasonably assumed, is based on the Sumerian poem, Gilgamesh and his loyal follower Enkidu succeeded in killing the "Bull of Heaven."[4] If so, this is one of the rare cases in Sumerian literature when the goddess suffered a humiliating defeat.

Turning to the myths, we find Inanna as a major protagonist in quite a number of them—the mythographers do not weary singing her daring, cunning, vindictive feats and exploits. One mythographer, for example, records that, having made up her mind to make her city Erech the center of civilized life, she set out on a dangerous journey to the *Abzu*, the deep abyss, where Enki had his watery abode and where he guarded those precious universal divine laws known as *me*, in order to transfer them from Eridu to Erech. To achieve her goal, she partakes of a banquet which Enki had especially prepared to celebrate her visit. In the course of this banquet there was much drinking, and she took advantage of this, to beguile and befuddle Enki, god of wisdom though he was, into turning over to her all the *me*, one at a time. After recovering from his drunken stupor, and realizing to his dismay that he had been duped, he dispatched all sorts of terrifying sea-monsters against Inanna, who was transporting the *me* in her boat, known as the "Boat of Heaven." But to no avail—the goddess succeeded in landing her precious cargo in Erech and unloading it safely.[5] In spite of this deceitful act, Enki, to judge from several myths, remained ever friendly and gracious to the goddess, even when at times he had to suffer from her reproachful complaints.

In another myth, Inanna is depicted as the vengeful goddess of

4. That the Akkadian Epic of Gilgamesh is based largely on Sumerian sources is demonstrated by my detailed comparative study published in the *Journal of the American Oriental Society*, vol. 64 (1944), pp. 7–23.

5. This is the myth recently edited by Gertrud Farber-Flügge; see footnote 7, Chapter 1, this volume.

war who with her fiery weapons virtually destroys Mt. Ebih, a region to the north of Sumer that had failed to do her homage. The introductory passage to this myth, a paean of glorification of In-anna as the goddess of war and as the bright Venus planet, is well worth quoting:

Lordly queen of the awesome *me*, garbed in fear, who rides the great *me*,
Inanna, you who have perfected the *a-ankara* weapon, who are covered with its blood,
Who storm about in great battles, who step upon shields,
Who initiate the flood-storm,
5 Great queen Inanna who are knowledgeable in planning combat,
Destroyer of *kur*, who have shot far the arrow from your arm, who have planted your arm upon the *kur*,
Like a lion you roared in heaven and earth, you smote the flesh of the people,
Like a big wild-ox you stood up eager to battle the inimical *kur*,
Like an awesome lion you annihilated with your venom the hostile and the disobedient.

10 My queen, when you become immense as heaven,
Maid Inanna, when you become vast as earth,
When you rise like King Utu, swinging wide your arms,
When you stand in heaven, garbed in your awesome fear,
When on earth you are garbed in bright, steadfast light,
15 When journeying over the mountains you come forth like a lapis-lazuli blue net,
When you bathe in the fruitful *kur*,
When you give birth to the bright *kur*, the pure *kur*,
When you seat yourself like a seemly lord, like a good lord,
When in their battles you lift high their heads like a devastating weapon,
20 Then the black-haired people break out in song,

All the lands utter sweetly their *ilulamma*-chant,
Queen of battle, great daughter of Sin,
Maid Inanna, I would praise you as is fitting.[6]

The vindictive aspect of Inanna's character is also attested in a myth that may be entitled "Inanna and Shukalletuda: The Gardener's Mortal Sin," a poem based primarily on a tablet in the Istanbul Museum of the Ancient Orient that I copied many years ago, and that has been recently published in volume 2 of the series *Sumerian Literary Tablets and Fragments in the Archaeological Museum of Istanbul*. The victim of Inanna's wrath in this myth is a gardener by the name of Shukalletuda, who raped the goddess while she was lying wearily under one of his shade trees, resting after her prolonged journey over the universe. To avenge this brazen, sacrilegious deed, she pursued him relentlessly and finally caught up with him and put him to death. But she seems not to have been totally displeased with his ardent passion, sacrilegious though it was, for she graciously consoled him by promising to have his name remembered in story and song.[7]

The contrasting strands in Inanna's multifaceted character are vividly apparent in her relations with her lover and husband, the shepherd-king Dumuzi, whom she wedded in the course of a joyous Sacred Marriage ritual, in order that, as the goddess of fertility and fecundity, she could ensure the productivity of the land and the fruitfulness of the womb of man and beast. Before the wedding, there was considerable courting and wooing between the sacred couple, according to the poets, who seem to have been fancy-free in inventing and elaborating the relevant details.[8] Thus,

6. For the translation of this passage, which is based on an unpublished manuscript in the University Museum, edited by Barry Eichler, note the following: the *a-ankara* (line 2) weapon is not identifiable at present; for the diverse meanings of *kur* (lines 6, 8, 16, 17), see footnote 9, Chapter 2, this volume.

7. An edition of this myth is now being prepared in the University Museum by Sol Cohen, one of my former students.

8. For bibliographical references, see *The Sacred Marriage Rite*, pp. 67–84, where a much fuller presentation of the texts concerned with the courting of Dumuzi and Inanna can be found.

according to one poet, it was the goddess who took the initiative, proclaiming in her own words,

I cast my eye over all the people,
Called Dumuzi to the godship of the land,
Dumuzi, the beloved of Enlil,
My mother holds him dear,
My father exalts him.

Then, continues the poet, she bathed, dressed in her special garments of power, and had Dumuzi brought to her shrine to rejoice at her side. His presence so fills her with passion and desire that then and there she composes a song for her vulva, comparing it to a horn, to the "Boat of Heaven," to the new crescent moon, to fallow land, to a high field, to a hillock, and concludes by exclaiming,

As for me, my vulva,
For me, the piled high hillock,
Me, the Maid, who will plow it for me?
My vulva, the watered ground—for me,
Me, the Queen, who will station the ox there?

To which the answer comes,

Oh lovely Lady, the king will plow it for you,
Dumuzi, the king, will plow it for you.

And joyfully she responds,

Plow my vulva, man of my heart.

After bathing her holy lap, they cohabit, and as expected vegetation flourishes all about them.

According to another poem that may be entitled "Love Finds a Way" or "Fooling Mother,"[9] the couple met by chance and fell

9. Inanna's mother was Ningal, the wife of the moon-god Nanna-Sin, and Dumuzi (also known as Kuli-anna, "Friend of An," Kuli-Enlil, "Friend of Enlil," and Ushumgal-anna, "Great Viper of Heaven") was therefore the son-in-law of the

passionately in love at first glance. This tender and ardent love lyric begins with Inanna soliloquizing:

Last night, as I the queen was shining bright,
Last night, as I the Queen of Heaven was shining bright,
Was shining bright, was dancing about,
Was uttering a chant at the brightening of the oncoming light,
5 He met me, he met me,
The lord Kuli-anna met me,
The lord put his hand into my hand,
Ushumgal-anna embraced me.

To be sure, she claims she tried to free herself from his embrace, since she did not know what to tell her mother:

Come now, wild bull, set me free, I must go home,
Kuli-Enlil, set me free, I must go home,
What can I say to deceive my mother,
What can I say to deceive my mother Ningal?

But Dumuzi had the answer that Inanna, noted for her frequent deceits, was only too happy to hear from his lips:

Let me inform you, let me inform you,
Inanna, most deceitful of women, let me inform you,
Say my girlfriend took me with her to the public square,
There she entertained me with music and dancing,
5 Her chant, so sweet, she sang for me,
In sweet rejoicing I whiled away the time there.
Thus cheerfully stand up to your mother,
While we by the moonlight indulge our passion,
I will prepare for you a bed pure, sweet, and noble,
10 Will while away sweet time with you in plenty and joy.

And Dumuzi evidently so relished the savor of Inanna's love that he must have promised to make her his rightful spouse. For the poem ends with the goddess singing ecstatically,

---

moon-god. He was also the brother-in-law of the sun-god Utu, since Utu and Inanna were the children of Nanna-Sin.

I have come to our mother's gate,
I, in joy I walk,
I have come to Ningal's gate,
I, in joy I walk.
5 To my mother he will say the word,
He will sprinkle cypress oil on the ground,
To my mother Ningal he will say the word,
He will sprinkle cypress oil on the ground—
He whose dwelling is fragrant,
10 Whose word brings deep joy.

While these two poems leave the impression that Dumuzi was Inanna's passionate, enthusiastic, one-and-only choice for husband-to-be, there is another poem that tells quite a different story: Inanna actually rejects the shepherd Dumuzi for his rival, the farmer Enkimdu, and it takes no little argument and suasion on the part of Dumuzi to induce her to change her mind. According to another poem, the goddess had some misgivings about his pedigree, and Dumuzi had to convince her that it was every bit as good as hers. But finally the marriage did take place and was celebrated with joyous music and song. What this marriage meant to the king of Sumer, and to the land and its people, can be gleaned from one of the "Sacred Marriage" poems which depicts Inanna's faithful vizier, a deity by the name of Ninshubur, leading Dumuzi, or the king conceived as Dumuzi incarnate, to the bride's lap, uttering a plea for the prosperity and well-being of the ruler and his people in these resounding, all-embracing words:

May the Lord whom you have called to your heart,
The king your beloved husband, enjoy long days at your lap, so
    sweet,
Give him a reign goodly and glorious,
Give him the throne of kingship on an enduring foundation,
5 Give him the people-directing scepter, the staff, and the crook,
Give him an enduring crown, a radiant diadem on his head,

Adoration

From where the sun rises to where the sun sets,
From south to north,
From the Upper Sea to the Lower Sea,
10   From the land of the *huluppu*-tree to the land of the cedar,
Over all Sumer and Akkad give him the staff and the crook,
May he exercise the shepherdship of the black-haired people
      wherever they dwell,
As the farmer may he make productive the fields,
As the shepherd may he multiply the sheepfolds.

15   Under his reign may there be vegetation, may there be grain,
In the field may there be rich grain,
In the marshland may the fish and birds chatter,
In the canebrake may the old reeds and young reeds grow high,
In the steppe may the *mashgur*-tree grow high
20   In the forests may the deer and wild goats multiply,
May the orchards produce honey and wine,
In the garden-beds may lettuce and cress grow high,
In the palace may there be long life,
In the Tigris and Euphrates may there be floodwater,
25   On the banks may plants grow high, may they fill the meadows,
May the grain-goddess pile high the grain in heaps and
      mounds.[10]

But there was one fatal flaw to this otherwise idyllic marriage, a
pitfall that Inanna knew, but about which she did not inform
Dumuzi until it was too late: it was law divine that no mortal could
love the goddess and live. In the sombre words of the goddess,

Your right hand you have placed on my vulva,
Your left stroked my head,
You have touched your mouth to mine,

10. For bibliographical references, see *The Sacred Marriage Rite*, pp. 82–83.
For the *huluppu*-tree (line 10), see footnote 5 of Chapter 1; the *mashgur*-tree (line
20) is still unidentifiable.

81

You have pressed my lips to your head,
That is why you are ill-fated.[11]

The story of the death of Dumuzi is told in the myth "Inanna's Descent to the Nether World," which I have reconstructed piece by piece over the past forty years from more than a score of tablets and fragments. Very briefly, the plot of the myth, which illuminates the ambitious and vindictive aspects of the goddess, may be sketched as follows:[12]

Inanna, though already the acknowledged "Queen of Heaven," makes up her mind to become mistress of the Nether World as well. Not unaware of the gravity of her decision, she arrays herself in dazzling garments and glittering ornaments indicative of her vast powers and prerogatives, and descends to the Lower Regions. However, the Queen of the Nether World, Ereshkigal by name, is not at all impressed by the goddess and her resplendent raiment, and has her put to death as an unwelcome and unauthorized intruder. But Enki, the god of wisdom comes to her rescue and manages to have her revived with the help of the "food of life" and the "water of life" that are under his charge.

The resurrected Inanna is now ready to leave the Nether World and ascend to the earth to visit her cities and temples. Unfortunately for the goddess, there was an unbroken law in the Nether World that no one, neither god nor man, could leave it unless they shall have produced a substitute to take their place. Inanna promises to do so, but the Queen of the Nether World does not trust her to keep her promise. She nevertheless allows Inanna to reascend to earth, but has her accompanied by the ghoulish little devils of the Lower Regions, with instructions to bring her back if she fails to provide a substitute.

Inanna reascends to the earth and wanders from city to city and from temple to temple. At each stop, the principal deity of the city,

11. These lines are part of a composition translated in *The Sacred Marriage Rite*, pp. 104–106.
12. For a translation and detailed analysis of the myth, see ibid., pp. 107–121.

on seeing the mighty and proud Inanna in the company of this ghoulish retinue, dresses in sackcloth and grovels at the feet of the suffering goddess. The little devils are only too eager to seize these deities one by one and carry them off to the Nether World as Inanna's surrogate, but the goddess, deeply touched by their tears of adoration and veneration, does not permit it. Finally she comes to her own city Erech, and there, to her chagrin, she finds her husband Dumuzi "dressed in noble garments," "sitting on a lofty throne," acting high and mighty—not for him weeping and lamenting and groveling in the dust at the heartbreaking scene of his spouse surrounded by clamoring demons and ghouls. This so incenses Inanna that

She fastened upon him the eye of death,
Spoke the word against him, the word of wrath,
Uttered the cry against him, the cry of guilt,

and, with no more ado, turned him over to the devils who bound, beat, tortured him, and carried him off to the infernal regions. And there he would have stayed forever and ever had not his beloved sister Geshtinanna made the supreme sacrifice, offering to take his place in the Nether World half the year, thus enabling Dumuzi to reascend to the earth every half year.

Not all the poets seemed to agree that it was Inanna who brought about the death of Dumuzi. Thus, according to a myth commonly known as "Inanna and Bilulu,"[13] the goddess did not know of the death of her spouse at all, until one day she came to visit his sheepfold and was informed that Dumuzi was dead, and that "a man who was not a shepherd" was bringing back the goddess's dispersed sheep. Then and there, according to the poet:

The queen gave birth to a song for her husband, fashioned a
    song for him,

13. This myth, inscribed on a tablet that I copied in Istanbul more than thirty years ago, was edited by Thorkild Jacobsen in the *Journal of Near Eastern Studies*, vol. 12 (1953), pp. 160–168.

Holy Inanna gave birth to a song for Dumuzi, fashioned a song
  for him:
"Oh you who are lying, Oh shepherd who are lying, you
  had stood watch over them,
Oh Dumuzi who are lying, Oh shepherd who are lying, you had
  stood watch over them,
5 Rising with the sun, you stood watch over them,
Lying down by night, you stood watch over my sheep."

Dumuzi's death in the steppe, according to this poet, seemed to
have been caused by a vicious crone by the name of Bilulu, upon
whom Inanna wreaks vengeance by putting her to death and
transforming her body into a water-skin, in order to refresh with
cold water all who roam the steppe, and thus "make sweet the
sleeping place" of her beloved and lamented Dumuzi.

Inanna was celebrated and glorified not only in epic and myth,
but also in a vast hymnal repertoire consisting of a varied assortment of psalms, lyrics, and chants as well as numerous dirges and
threnodies relating primarily to the death of her lover and husband,
the shepherd-king Dumuzi. In these hymnal compositions, as in
the epics and myths, the goddess emerges as a complex, manysided
personality embodying contrasting attitudes and contradictory
characteristics.

Here, for example, are two passage from a hymn to the goddess as
the Morning Star and Evening Star that are vivid witness to the
profound feeling of adoration and reverence on the part of the
Sumerian people for their beloved "Queen of Heaven." This
hymn, inscribed primarily on tablets and fragments excavated by
the University of Pennsylvania almost a century ago, had been
known in part for some time. In 1969, the text of the hymn, with
translation and commentary, was edited by Daniel Reisman in a
doctoral dissertation prepared for the Department of Oriental
Studies, under the supervision and guidance of my successor as
Curator of the Tablet Collection, Åke Sjöberg, and my translation is based on this edition. The first passage, which depicts the

Adoration

adoration of the goddess as the Evening Star by all living creatures
and even by the verdant vegetation, reads as follows:

The holy one stands all alone in the clear sky;
Upon all the lands and upon the black-haired people, the people
    as numerous as sheep,
The Lady looks in sweet wonder from heaven's midst;
They parade before the holy Inanna,
5 The Lady of the Evening, Inanna, is lofty,
The Maid, Inanna, I would praise as is fitting,
The Lady of the Evening is lofty on the horizon.

At evening, the radiant star, the great light that fills the sky,
The Lady of the Evening comes forth bravely from heaven,
10 The people in all the lands lift their eyes to her,
The men purify themselves, the women cleanse themselves,
The ox in his yoke lows to her,
The sheep pile up the dust in their fold,
The beasts of Sumugan, the multitudinous living creatures of
    the steppe,
15 The four-legged creatures of the high steppe,
The lush orchards and gardens, the verdant reeds and trees,
The fish of the deep, the birds of heaven,
The Lady makes them hurry to their sleeping places.

The living creatures, the multitudinous people, bend the knee
    before her,
20 The "called ones" of the matriarchs, for the Queen,
Prepare immense quantities of food and drink,
The Lady refreshes herself in the land,
There is festive play in the land,
The young man soothes the heart of his spouse.

25 My Lady looks on in wonder from heaven's midst,
They parade before the holy Inanna,

The Lady of the Evening, Inanna, is lofty,
The Maid, Inanna, I would praise as is fitting,
The Lady of the Evening is lofty on the horizon.[14]

The second passage relates to the moral and ethical aspects of the
goddess in her epiphany as Morning Star. As the poet imagined it,
the people everywhere, on waking in the morning, come to the
goddess for judgment and approbation, and Inanna, after studying their "words," distinguishes between the righteous and the
wrongdoer, rewarding the one and punishing the other. Or as the
poet puts it,

She made the night come forth like the moonlight,
She made the morning come forth like the bright daylight,
When in the bed-chamber sweet sleep had come to an end,
When all the lands and the black-haired people had
　　assembled—
5 Who had slept on the roofs, who had slept in the walls—
And uttering orisons approached her, brought their words to her,
Then did she study their words, knew the evildoer,
Against the evildoer she renders a cruel judgment, she destroys
　　the wicked,
She looks with kindly eyes on the straightforward, gives him her
　　blessing.

10 My Lady looks on in sweet wonder from heaven's midst,
They parade before the holy Inanna,
The Lady who reaches heaven, Inanna, is lofty,
The Maid, Inanna, I would praise as is fitting.

In stark contrast to this idealized portrait of the bright, shining,
lovable, adorable goddess is a passage that introduces a hymnal
prayer by Enheduanna, the high-priestess of the temple of the

14. In this translated passage note the following: Sumugan (line 14) is the god in
charge of the steppes and its living creatures; the meaning of line 20 is not clear;
"soothe the heart" (line 24) is a euphemism for sexual intercourse.

moon-god Nanna, who for some unstated reason had incurred Inanna's displeasure and wrath.[15] In this passage, the goddess is depicted as a cruel, destructive, vindictive deity, venomous and tempestuous; a raging, thundering, stormy goddess before whom all mankind trembles and quakes; an irate, relentless, intractable goddess of war before whom even the great gods, the Anunna, flee in terror. The poetess begins pleasantly enough:

> Queen of all the *me*, radiant light,
> Life-giving woman, beloved of Heaven and Earth,
> Hierodule of An, much bejeweled,
> Who loves the life-giving tiara, fit for the high-priesthood,
> 5 Who grasps in her hand the seven *me*.
> My Queen, you who are the guardian of all the great *me*,
> You have lifted the *me*, have tied the *me* to your hands,
> Have gathered the *me*, pressed the *me* to your breast.

But she then continues with this devastating description:

> You have filled the land with venom like a dragon,
> 10 Vegetation ceases when you thunder like Ishkur,[16]
> You who bring down the Flood from the mountain,
> Supreme one, who are the queen of heaven and earth,
> Who rain flaming fire over the land,
> Who have been given the *me* by An, Queen who rides the
>   beasts,
> 15 Who at the holy command of An, utters the words (divine),
> Who can fathom your great ordinances!

> Destroyer of the foreign lands, you have given wings to the
>   storm,

15. This myth has been edited by William Hallo and J. J. Van Dijk in a monograph entitled *The Exaltation of Inanna* (1968); for a translation that differs in some respects from the Hallo-van Dijk version, see *Ancient Near Eastern Texts*, pp. 579–581.

16. Ishkur is the god of winds and storms.

Beloved of Enlil, you made it blow over the land,
You carried out the instructions of An.

20 My Queen, the foreign lands cower at your cry,
In dread and fear of you, the South Wind,
Mankind brought you their anguished clamor,
Took before you their anguished outcry,
Set up before you wailing and weeping,
25 Brought before you the great lamentations in the city streets,

In the heat of battle, everything was struck down before you,
My Queen, you are all-devouring in your power,
You kept on attacking like the attacking storm,
Kept on blowing louder than the howling storm,
30 Kept on moaning louder than the evil winds,
Your feet grew not weary,
You caused wailing to resound on the harp of lament.

My Queen, the Anunna, the great gods,
Fled before you like fluttering bats,
35 Could not stand before your awesome face,
Could not approach your awesome forehead.
Who can soothe your angry heart!

For the past several summers I have had the privilege of studying some of the unpublished Sumerian literary tablets and fragments in the British Museum, and among them I identified quite a number relating to Inanna.[17] One of these, BM 23820, is a small tablet inscribed in minute cuneiform with a hymnal prayer to the goddess for Ishme-Dagan, a king who reigned about 1900 B.C. I should like to cite three extracts from this composition, each reflecting a different aspect of Inanna's personality. The poet begins with a portrayal of Inanna as the goddess of wrath and destruction, thus:

17. Editions of the British Museum texts mentioned in the pages that follow are now being prepared by me for future publication.

Adoration

Queen of the earth-gods, proud, supreme among the
    heaven-gods,
Inanna, who pours down rain over all the lands, over all the
    people, loud-thundering storm,
Hierodule, who makes heavens tremble, who makes the earth
    quake,
Who can soothe your heart?
5 You who pour down firebrands over the earthly orb, who flash
    like lightning over the highland,
South Wind, whose deafening command splits asunder the great
    mountains,
You who trample the disobedient like a wild bull, who make
    heaven and earth tremble, who are the consternation of the
    land,
Whose cry reaches heaven and earth, whose roar is
    all-destructive,
Your earth-shuddering hand brings the midday heat over the sea,
10 When you stalk the heavens in the dark night, all the people are
    chilled by the breeze,
Your angry heart is a terrifying flood-wave that overflows all the
    river banks.

After continuing in this fearful vein for another fifty lines or so,
the poet has a complete change of heart, as he proceeds to portray
the goddess sitting on her lofty dais on the seventh day of each
month when the moon lights up the sky:

On the seventh day when the crescent moon has reached its
    monthly fullness,
You bathed, poured fresh water ritually over your holy
    countenance,
Covered your body with the long woolen garments of queenship,
Fastened battle and combat to your side, tied them into a girdle,
5 Seated yourself high on the lofty dais, made known there your
    broad authority,

89

Inanna, you seated there your beloved husband at your side,[18]
The gods of the land came before you that you might decree
   their fate,
The gods of the heavenly orb, of the earthly orb, seated
   themselves before you,
Upon the living creatures, upon the black-haired people in their
   multitude, who came before you,
10 You lifted your eyes as their goddess, you made them bear your
   holy yoke.

Following an itemization of Inanna's vast cult-personnel, the poet
introduces the king Ishme-Dagan as a tragic, suffering, heart-bro-
ken individual, and pleads with the goddess to accept the prayers
and invocations of the king's personal god[19] and to transfer her
wrath and punishment to the king's rebellious enemies, whose
transgressions are myriad. He then concludes with these lines,

She accepted the prayer he had uttered,
The Queen of the searching eye, the guide of the land, the
   all-compassionate,
Removed from that man the bruising cane that had been laid
   upon him,
Attacking on his behalf the demons of disease and sickness, she
   extirpated them from that man,
5 The whip that had been laid cruelly upon him she made into a
   cloth bandage,
She made the silver-ore as bright as good silver, purified it,
She gazed upon him with joyous heart, gave him life,
She returned him to the gracious hand of his god,
Placed the ever-present good angels at his head,
10 Had Utu provide him with truth, dressed him with it like a lion,
Blessed his womb, gave him an heir,

18. The "beloved husband" refers to Dumuzi.
19. For the role of the personal god in Sumerian religion, see *The Sumerians,*
pp. 126–129.

Gave him a spouse who bore him a son, spread wide his stalls
  and sheepfolds,
Gave him a faithful household, decreed a sweet fate for him.

The wrath and fury of Inanna troubled not only mankind and
the lesser gods of the Sumerian pantheon, but the leading deities as
well, and one of them, Enki, the god of wisdon, decided to do
something about it. This is told in a mythological passage that is
part of an hitherto unknown poem inscribed on the tablet now
catalogued as BM 29616. The poet sets the stage for Enki's salutary
intervention with such exclamatory remonstrating lines addressed
to Inanna as

What has your heart wrought? How you torment heaven and
  earth!
Hierodule, what has your heart wrought? How you torment
  heaven and earth!
What has your furious heart wrought? How you torment heaven
  and earth!
What has your heart, furious as the floodwater, wrought? How you
  torment heaven and earth!

When Enki heard this cry, the poet continues, he took counsel
with himself and fashioned the temple singer known as *gala*, put
him in charge of a varied assortment of chants, prayers, and
laments, and placed in his hand the tambourine and the kettle-
drum. He then sent a messenger to the goddess, who urged her to sit
down calmly on her throne while the *gala* soothed her with the
chants that bring peace to the spirit.

As is evident from this poem and from several long-known
myths, Inanna was a high favorite of the god Enki. But she had
her troubles with Enki's superior, Enlil, the supreme deity of the
Sumerian pantheon. This is vividly depicted in a lament by the
goddess inscribed on the tablet now catalogued as BM 96679, in

which she accuses Enlil of having caused her much grief and despair. Or, as the poet puts it,

He has filled me with dismay, he has filled me with
    consternation,
Me, the woman, he has filled with dismay, he has filled with
    consternation,
The mighty one has filled me with dismay, has filled me with
    consternation,
The lord Enlil, the king of the land,
5 Has filled me, the queen of heaven, with consternation,
Me, the hierodule of An, the queen of heaven,
Who destroys all inimical lands, the queen of Eanna,
Who makes the heavens tremble, the queen of the sacred
    temple-grove,
The most mighty one, the queen of stall and fold,
10 Father Enlil has filled me with consternation in my city,
Has filled me with consternation in my city Erech.

Following a long fragmentary passage with a recurrent bitter refrain "Whither shall I go?," the poet continues with a picture of the goddess seated before Enlil in his temple, beseeching him with a persistent demand for an answer to her bitter, plaintive queries:

I—tell me where is my house,
I, the woman who circles the land—tell me where is my house,
Tell me where is the city in which I may live,
Tell me where is the house in which I may rest at ease.
5 Oh Enlil, I, who am your daughter—tell me where is my
    house,
I, the hierodule who am your bridesmaid—tell me where is my
    house,[20]
I, the queen of heaven, who am dear to your heart—tell me
    where is my house,

20. The meaning of this line is not clear.

Adoration

Tell me where is my house, my mute, silent house,
My house in which a spouse no longer lives, in which I no
    longer greet a son,
10 I, the queen of heaven, am one in whose house a spouse no
    longer lives, in whose house I no longer greet a son.

The bird has its nesting place, but I—my young are dispersed,
The fish lies in calm waters, but I—my resting place exists not,
The dog kneels at the threshold, but I—I have no threshold,
The ox has a stall, but I—I have no stall,
15 The cow has a place to lie down, but I—I have no place to lie
    down,
The ewe has a fold, but I—I have no fold,
The beasts have a place to sleep, but I—I have no place to
    sleep.

As already noted, Inanna was the major protagonist in a Sacred
Marriage ritual that celebrated the sexual union between the goddess and her lover, the shepherd-king Dumuzi, sometimes designated in the texts as her brother. This ritual marriage, according to
the belief of the theologians and poets, ensured the rich harvest of
cereals and legumes that were the prime source of food for the
Sumerian people. A concrete and graphic expression of this credo
is found in a passage that is part of a Dumuzi-Inanna composition
inscribed on the tablet now catalogued as BM 88318, which has
the goddess chanting,

He made me enter, he made me enter,
My brother made me enter his garden,
Dumuzi made me enter his garden,
He made me approach with him a high grove,
5 Made me stand with him by a high bed.

Steadily I kneel by an apple tree,
My brother comes chanting,

93

The lord Dumuzi comes up to me,
Comes up to me out of the reddish oak-leaves,
10 Comes up to me out of the midday heat—
I pour out before him legumes from my womb,
I bring into being legumes before him, I pour out legumes
  before him,
I bring into being grains before him, I pour out grains before
  him.

Finally there is the tablet BM 23631, inscribed with two hymns to the sun-god Utu, which contains a mythological passage that reveals a facet of Inanna's character hitherto unknown and hardly suspected—her innocence in the matter of sex. The passage, consisting of the last thirty-five lines of the tablet, begins with a narrative statement that Inanna's brother, the sun-god Utu, was providing beer for himself and his sister in a tavern—"a wine house"—far from his home-ground, the Cedar mountain to the east, the Sumerian Olympus. Just why Utu was spending his time drinking with his sister in a tavern is not stated in the text. But from Inanna's address, which follows, it may be inferred that he was doing so in an attempt to seduce his sister. In the course of this speech she pleads with her brother, saying that she would like to "ride" with him to the Cedar mountain, but that she knows nothing about sexual intercourse, and that after they had eaten of the aromatic herbs and cedars of the mountain he should not detain her, but send her back home to her family, for after all he was a compassionate god, a defender and protector of the wanderer and the homeless, of the orphan and the widow. Here now is a translation of virtually the entire passage.

Utu provided beer at the tavern,
Valiant Utu provided beer at the tavern.
My brother, awesome lord, I would ride with you to the
  mountain,

Adoration

Lord of heaven, awesome lord, I would ride with you to the
    mountain,
5 To the mountain of aromatic herbs, to the mountain of
    cedars—to the mountain,
To the mountain of cedars, to the mountain of
    hashur-cedars—to the mountain,
To the mountain of silver, to the mountain of lapis-lazuli—to
    the mountain,
To the mountain where exhilarating plants grow—to the
    mountain,
Where is the swift-flowing river whose waters gush out of the
    earth.

Following five lines that are fragmentary and unintelligible, the
poem continues as follows:

15 That which pertains to women—copulation—I know not,
That which pertains to women—kissing—I know not,
I know not copulation, I know not kissing,
At the mountain—whatsoever exists there let us eat,
At the mountain peak—whatsoever exists there, let us eat,
20 At the mountain of aromatic herbs, at the mountain of cedars,
At the mountain of cedars, at the mountain of *hashur*-cedars,
At the mountain—whatsoever exists there, let us eat.

After having eaten of the aromatic herbs, after having eaten of
    the cedars,
Hold my hand in your hand, send me back to my house,
25 Send me back to my house, send me back to my house in
    Zabalam,
Send me back to my mother, to my mother Ningal,
Send me back to my mother-in-law, to Ninsun,
Send me back to my sister-in-law, to Geshtinanna.

Of the wanderer, of the homeless,
30 Of the homeless, of the wanderer,
Utu, you are their mother, you, you are their father,
Utu—the orphan, Utu—the widow,
Utu, the orphan gazes up to you as his father,
Utu, you show favor to the widows like their mother. [21]

Loved by kings and heroes, glorified by poets and bards, adored by man and beast, Inanna is the very epitome of the liberated woman, the ideal divine patroness for the current "women's lib" movement. Bright, brave, ambitious, aggressive, vindictive, but lovable and desirable nonetheless, she allowed no one, neither man nor god, to stand in her way, say her nay. As she herself sums it up in a self-laudatory chant composed by some adoring bard,

My father gave me heaven, gave me earth,
I, the Queen of Heaven am I,
Is there a god who can vie with me?
Enlil gave me heaven, gave me earth,
5 I, the Queen of Heaven am I!
He has given me lordship,
He has given me queenship,
He has given me battle, he has given me combat,
He has given me the Flood, he has given me the Tempest,
10 He has placed heaven as a crown on my head,
He has tied the earth as a sandal at my foot,
He has fastened the holy garmet of the *me* about my body,
He has placed the holy scepter in my hand.

Following a passage in which she compares herself to a "life-giving wild cow" who lets no one get in her way when she enters Enlil's

21. In the translation of this passage, note the following: the *hashur* (lines 6 and 16) is an unidentifiable kind of cedar; Zabalam was the seat of one of Inanna's important shrines; Ninsun was the mother of Dumuzi, Inanna's spouse; Geshtinanna was Dumuzi's sister (see p. 83 of this manuscript).

great temple, the Ekur, the goddess proceeds to itemize all her important temples in the land, a list that is preceeded by the exclamatory line:

Heaven is mine, earth is mine—I, a warrior am I!

and is concluded with the challenging words:

Is there a god who can vie with me?[22]

22. Compare *Ancient Near Eastern Texts*, pp. 578–579.

Index

Index

Gudea, 2, 7, 59
Gudea Cylinders, 3
Gurney, Oliver, 11

Hallo, William, 11, 12, 87
Hammurabi, 58, 59, 60
Handbuch der Keilschriftliteratur, 11
Haupt, Paul, 2, 3
Heidelberger Studien zum Alten Orient, 11
Heimerdinger, Jane, 11
"Helen of Troy"-motif, 73
Hilprecht Anniversary Volume, 4
Hilprecht Sammlung, 10, 48
Historical and Grammatical Texts, 5
Historical and Religious Texts from the Temple Library of Nippur, 6
huluppu-tree, 22, 24, 74, 81

Iliad, 21
Imdugud-bird, 22, 23
Inanna (Semitic Ishtar), 2, 11, 22, 31, 32, 33, 36, 40, 48, 62, 67, 70; three aspects of, 71–73; role in epic tales, 73–75; in myths, 75–77; in Sacred Marriage ritual, 77–81; death of her husband Dumuzi, 81–84; role in hymns and hymnal prayers, 84–97
Inscriptions from Tell Abu Salabih, 7
Inscriptions of Western Asia, 1, 13
Inscriptions Royales Sumeriennes et Akkadiennes, 58
Intellectual Adventures of Ancient Man, 20
Iraq, 21, 53
Irrigation — importance of, 55–56
irshemma, 3, 13
Ishkur, 87
Ishme-Dagan, 62, 66, 67, 68, 88, 90
Ishtar. *See* Inanna

Isin, 51
Istanbul, 4, 7, 8, 83
Istanbul Arkeoloji Müzelerinde Bulunan Edibi Tabletler ve Parcalari, 10, 77

Jacobsen, Thorkild, 11, 15, 51, 56, 57, 83
Joint British Museum-University Museum Expedition, 10
Joint Oriental Institute-University Museum Expedition, 11
Jones, Tom, 51
Journal of the American Oriental Society, 75
Journal of Cuneiform Studies, 9, 20
Journal of Near Eastern Studies, 83

Ki (Mother Earth), 26, 27, 28, 31
King, L. W., 3
Kinglist, 57
Kingship: origin and development of, 50–59; stylistic features of royal hymns, 59–60; portrayal of ideal ruler, 60; divine birth, 60–61; divine blessings, 61–63; education and upbringing, 63–65; physical appearance and prowess, 65–67; wisdom of, 67; devotion to cult, 67–68; concern for social justice, 68; Sumerian perception of their kings, 68-69; the ideal Sumerian man, 69
Kish, 4, 7, 57
Kizilyay, Hatice, 10
Kramer Anniversary Volume, 11
Kraus, F. R., 57
Krecher, Joachim, 2, 5
Kuli-anna. *See* Dumuzi
Kuli-Enlil. *See* Dumuzi
Kullab, 51
Kupper, Jean Robert, 58
kur, 13, 24, 25, 38, 75

Lagash, 2, 51, 56
Lahar, 41, 42

Index